Glimpses
of a Good Life

Walter Thiessen

st. stephen's publishing

St. Stephen, NB Canada

Copyright © 2013 Walter Thiessen

All rights reserved.

ISBN-13: 978-0-9936245-0-6

Cover design: Cara Thiessen,
photos by W. Thiessen and W. Bernard

www.glimpsesofagoodlife.com

St. Stephen's Publishing
8 Main St.
St. Stephen, NB E3L 3E2

New Revised Standard Version Bible: Anglicized Edition, copyright 1989, 1995, Division of Christian Education of the National Council of the Churches of Christ in the United States of America. Used by permission. All rights reserved.

To all who are or have been a part of the communities
that have given my life a context and meaning, especially:
my family,
St. Stephen's University,
and St. Croix Vineyard

CONTENTS

	Introduction	1
1	Celebrating	9
2	Lamenting	21
3	Accepting	35
4	Good Work	59
5	Embracing the Other	77
6	Journeying Together	97
7	Yearning for Home	119

I was never in a hurry in my life. He lives long who enjoys life and bears no jealousy of others, whose heart harbours no malice or anger, who sings a lot and cries a little, who rises and retires with the sun, who likes to work, and who knows how to rest.

– Shirali Muslimov
[A shepherd in the village of Barzavu in Azerbaijan who died in 1973, allegedly at the age of 168]

If the world were merely seductive, that would be easy. If it were merely challenging, that would be no problem. But I arise in the morning torn between a desire to improve the world, and a desire to enjoy the world. This makes it hard to plan the day.

– E. B. White

The most precious goods are not to be sought out, but to be waited for (expectantly). For we cannot find them in our own power, and if we give ourselves to searching for them, we find false goods in their place that we cannot discern as falsities.

– Simone Weil (trans. B. Jersak)

INTRODUCTION

You are speeding down the freeway in your car, barely noticing the woods beside you, until you eventually feel like slowing down. So you take the exit, choosing the smaller road that winds alongside the forest. At this speed you notice occasional flickers of light as the late afternoon sun sparkles on a body of water on the other side of the trees. Intrigued, you park the car and, on foot, find a small path that enters the wood. This path runs parallel to the road, and now, at a human pace, you are able to catch regular glimpses of a beautiful blue lake occasionally making itself known through the trees.

My intent is to describe the possibility of living well, of wholeness, in a way that echoes that walk through the woods. Wholeness is not a state but a movement. A good life is not some distant goal that we are striving toward, nor should it be unattainable. I believe that we often live unaware of how near we are to catching glimpses of a life that feels right, somehow in tune with what is meant to be.

The ingredients of a good life are not wealth, ease, or bodily perfection; a good life requires, rather, that we have people to connect with and a world that offers up its natural and spiritual opportunities and challenges. This is good news because it means that wholeness is near enough for most of us to taste—even if we have mental or physical challenges, or live in a corner of the world with more than its share of violence, or subsist on the edge of hunger.

Yet most of us don't usually feel that wholeness is close. We yearn for a better way to live. For those of us who have not given up, this hope is what keeps us moving. For our own sake, for the sake of others, for the sake of the planet or the sake of God, we're convinced that more is possible.

At the same time, choosing contentment and acceptance have long been acknowledged as part of a richer life. So, at best, we are both driven and content, peacefully striving for a good life. Clearly this search, when at all successful, will lead us to a path characterized by such terms as balance, rhythm and paradox.

I'm not sure why I stumbled into a life that has focused on exploring wholeness from a pretty young age. I think of moments that awoke in me a longing for a richer life. My suburban childhood was secure and loving, but I don't take it as a coincidence that the times in my life as an adolescent that gave a taste of something deeper were away from the city with its typical institutions and technologies. I recall sitting around a campfire with strangers who had recently become friends, one of them playing guitar and singing, "Bridge Over Troubled Water." Or I think of canoe trips in the Canadian Shield, sunning on a huge granite boulder after a day of paddling and portages. Or, working as part of a team of very young, inexperienced, but idealistic camp staff, I remember heartfelt moments of mutual encouragement when we were on the verge of mental and physical exhaustion—what strikes me most when I recall this was how much that encouragement *mattered*.

Of course, I was also affected by seeing instances where wholeness was particularly absent. There was junior high with its boredom and bullying. There were Saturday afternoons wasted in front of a television that left me feeling empty and apathetic. There was a memorable loss of naiveté one Friday evening in my college years when, as an assignment for a counselling class, I rode along with a police cruiser after midnight in Winnipeg's North End: It was a quiet night and after an hour or two with nothing happening, the driver, concerned that my experience would be meaningless, flicked on his siren saying, "There's an Indian in a cowboy hat, let's check that out." Inside I burned with a sense of injustice at this prejudiced harassment, but then the intended victim took off, and we were on a brief car chase. We caught the car on a nearby side street, the very drunk driver pointlessly trying to switch places with his passenger. It turned out they had just robbed a gas bar, and I watched as the verbal and physical harassment switched directions, and was now aimed at the arresting officers. And this all happened because I was present. The brokenness of the system was a lot bigger and more complicated than one bigoted cop.

Somewhere out of these mixed experiences, I developed a hunger to understand more about what factors made it possible for one to live better. In my undergrad years this led to a focus on intentional communities, the power of narrative, and a fundamental need for both peace and justice. A few years later, a graduate program in counselling caught my eye, based on the relatively young science of family systems. My thesis explored the tension between individuality and healthy community that is crucial to wholeness. Later, my doctoral studies used narrative psychology to interpret ways in which imaginative prayer can lead to inner healing of traumatic memories and other forms of emotional woundedness.

As a counsellor for over 20 years now, I have also walked alongside a great many people in very different situations, all in some way seeking wholeness. While people are usually seeking some specific changes or improvements, I have found that the presence or lack of wholeness in the background contexts of their lives has a lot to do with the likelihood of clients reaching a satisfactory outcome.

I suspect my formal education and professional experiences alone would have led to fairly thin understandings, however, if I had not also been trying to live these things out in my own life with my family, a household that we have nearly always shared with boarders, and a rich community of friends and neighbours. Sharing life with real human beings in real communities is a great way to topple unhelpful images of perfection. It seems that any individuals or groups of people, once you get to know them, turn out to be a motley crew of diversity, beauty and brokenness.

So, the reflections of this book have grown out of a mixture of reading, contemplation and a life lived intentionally with others. What has emerged for me are seven broad rhythms or categories that make possible a good life. I am suggesting that there is a universality to these rhythms, in that they apply to and are accessible to everyone, regardless of education, culture, or access to resources. I hope this description will have at least some degree of fit for an artist in New York, a subsistence farmer in Ethiopia, a sweat shop worker in Bangladesh, or someone institutionalized with schizophrenia.

Each of the seven rhythms contains specific practices, which I don't presume to suggest are as universal as the rhythms themselves. The more specific and practical I get with these ideas, the more I intend them as examples that are interchangeable with a host of other possible examples and specifics for people living in different contexts.

I have also clustered the seven rhythms into two sets of three, followed by one final rhythm. The first three I call the "rhythms of response" because they represent the primary ways in which we respond to life: celebration, lament and acceptance. The second set of three I call the "rhythms of action": good work, the embrace of others and the journey together. Finally there is the seventh rhythm of yearning for home, which draws us through the other rhythms.

Paradoxes and tensions

I hope that by emphasizing the rhythmic quality to these practices that invite wholeness, I am making lots of room for paradox and tension. I even hope that some of my suggestions sound a bit contradictory; otherwise, I fear I would have missed the balance I am seeking. I believe this sense of paradox is biologically wired into humanity, with the left and right hemispheres of our brains enabling us to interact with our world in two very different ways: one focused and analytical and the other wide open, aware of what is threatening and what is possible. The first allows clarity; the second enables connection.

Readers immersed in North American individualism may feel like the rhythms outlined have a frustrating tendency to assume a shared life in community. I plead guilty to the bias, but I have also sought to ensure that individual boundaries and time alone are deeply respected. There is no magic synthesis to dissolve the tension between individual freedom and commitment to others. I feel this tension nearly every day since my personality would tend toward solitude, but my experience has taught me how much I need others.

Finally, there is a paradox in the relationship between spontaneity and structure. One of the main reasons for my title is that, for me, the word "glimpses" captures this tension, since glimpses catch us as much as we catch them.

Some structure is provided for us by daily or seasonal rhythms or by cultural expectations and traditions. But rarely will we sense that we are approaching wholeness until we add some intentionality and structure to the mix. In my individual, family and community life, I have discovered that without structure, it is impossible for me to live an intentional life. I simply will not spontaneously do the most important things in life. Laziness, forgetfulness, busyness and false urgencies all combine to squeeze out my best intentions except where I (or we) have found structures to which I (and others) are committed. Consistent, chosen rhythms have added an incredible richness to my life, and I have rarely regretted committing myself to such a rhythm for a season.

Yet, even in the midst of an intentional and structured life, the spontaneous moments that capture us by surprise are often the sweetest. So we want any rhythms that we structure into our lives to leave plenty of room for flexibility, creativity and space for the unexpected.

Getting Practical

The end of each chapter will suggest practical examples of how the ideas in that section might be lived out. The point is not to work through these suggestions like a workbook (most of us ignore those sections when we read anyway) but to allow the examples to stimulate our own creative ways to embody the practices and rhythms discussed.

Community assessment: To get the ball rolling, I want to invite one direct, practical step. Consider one of the tensions just mentioned: between the individual and the community. Take a couple of moments to ask yourself how you are doing with that balance. Are you struggling with one or both of these areas? Are you a part of a community that supports and provides a meaningful context for your individual and family life? Do you get time alone to really consider in silence how your life is going for you? Are both sides missing as your life pulls you away from both meaningful relationship *and* time alone? Don't just let the question hang there—articulate a clear answer in your head (if you feel like it, write it down), and then let that thought play in the back of your mind as you read the rest of this book.

THE RESPONSIVE RHYTHMS

The Responsive Rhythms

The first three rhythms reflect our basic responses to life: to the world we inhabit, to the people around us, to the situations in which we find ourselves, to God. I label these rhythms as celebration, lament and acceptance.

These responsive rhythms are all interconnected, even overlapping. Celebration is our acceptance and engagement with the good and the beautiful. We give thanks for, partake in, and take note of that which calls forth affirmation. If we don't celebrate, we deny the reality of the deep beauty in the world. We must give voice to our "yes" about all that is right in the world.

Likewise, lament is the expression of our journey to accept the reality of suffering and pain. As we lament we sort out the realities we fight to change and the realities we know we must accept. Either way we admit the reality of that which troubles us, smites us and oppresses us. The shout, the dirge, the sorrowful song are the cries of the heart as denial gives way to truth. So the lament gives us courage—courage to work for change or courage to submit.

Strands of acceptance, are woven through all the responsive rhythms and, in a sense, sum them up. We enter into a deep honesty in how we face life, with all of its challenges and limits, coming to peace with it all.

All three of the responsive rhythms invite us to deepen our experience. Too often the distractions of our contemporary world tempt us to skitter around on the surface of things. Paying attention to these three rhythms can help us to engage more fully and intentionally with all of life.

1 CELEBRATING

*Every real thing is a joy, if only you have
eyes and ears to relish it,
a nose and a tongue to taste it.*

– Robert Farrar Capon

*I think it pisses God off if you walk by the color purple in a field
somewhere and don't notice it.
What it do when it pissed off? I ast.
Oh, it make something else. People think pleasing God is all God
care about. But any fool living in the world can see it always
trying to please us back.
Yeah? I say.
Yeah, she say. It always making little surprises
and springing them on us when us least expect.
You mean it want to be loved, just like the bible say.
Yes, Celie, she say. Everything want to be loved.*

– dialogue in Alice Walker's *The Color Purple*

Imagine walking into a community hall in a small town where a banquet is just having its main course cleared away. While the desserts are being served, the hostess of the evening steps up to the microphone, and you realize the room is filled to standing room only in order to honour the retirement of the janitor of the town's youth centre.

Guests nibble away at delicate crepes folded over moist bits of brownie, slathered with whipped cream, sprinkled with toasted almonds and capped off with a drizzle of pure dark chocolate. In between savoured bites, they listen to several speakers of various ages, sharing memories and poking respectful fun at the elderly janitor. You come to realize this was no ordinary janitor. He's remembered because he seemed to know the name of every kid who ever passed through the doors of the youth centre. He was a man who knew how to pay attention.

You hear about the times when someone new would occasionally question how well he used his time, since he was so often chatting with the teens, teasing them, encouraging them. But those concerned had always been silenced when the questioner realized the building was kept in spotless shape. You hear how youths getting into trouble were often "sentenced" to community service under his care, receiving more kindness and wisdom working alongside the humble man than they would receive from any counsellor. You start to guess that many of the people in the room had grown up affected by his example.

After tumultuous applause, the man himself steps up to the podium. During his brief response, he shares, by way of contrast, just a few details of an early life of much pain and loneliness, ending with a simple thanks for all the trust that had been placed in him over the years and for the opportunity to devote himself to a task that was so meaningful. There are few dry eyes.

~

Perhaps more than anything else, those who are approaching wholeness can be spotted by their ability to celebrate the fullness of life even while suffering hardships or facing challenges. Celebration represents the rightness of engaging with and responding to the world and each other with gratitude and affirmation. When we celebrate something we pay particular attention to it, honouring, remembering and taking note with a wide variety of expression. Celebration is delighting in the full reality of life with all its "warts and wrinkles."

In the Judeo-Christian story about the origins of the world, we read that God's first response to creation was that "it was good." Celebration is the first and foundational orientation toward life.

At the same time, the tale of Adam and Eve is as natural a place as any to be reminded of how quickly less-than-good elements enter the picture, complicating our ongoing practice of celebration. These complications—including the pain and suffering that are part of life—actually intensify the need for, and power of, celebration. I recall waking up to this when reading *City of Joy* by Dominique Lapierre, in which he recounts the power of celebration among some of the world's poorest people in Calcutta, who chose to risk malnutrition rather than sell their festive garments. Our need to celebrate, in spite of or because of the difficulties of life, runs deep.

Celebrating the natural world

In spite of the complications, most of us will feel an innate and intuitive response of celebration to the natural world. Whether triggered by a "mundane" example like a blade of grass or an overwhelming vista of snow-capped mountains, wonder and gratitude are responses that well up from deep within us as we pay attention to the natural world. The urge to celebrate this inner response is not based on a naïve belief in nature being "nice." We celebrate knowing the destruction of which our earth is capable and the cycles of life and death upon which the ecosystem is based. Natural beauty can be still and lovely or wild and fierce.

Time and again, I am amazed at the ability of an encounter with nature to heal and create a sense of spiritual connection. The exercise I most frequently give students and counselling clients is to take a "walk into peace." The primary instructions for a short walk in as natural a setting as possible are to give complete attention to one's physical senses and to practise an attitude of curiosity. While the results of this exercise may sometimes be fleeting, most people experience a taste of clarity and peace as their usual cacophony of thoughts gives way to simple appreciation.

Celebrating the natural world is closely tied to celebrating our physical senses and their response to either natural or human creation. We delight in the colours of flowers, the composition of a painting, the smile on a child's face. We listen in wonder to a Beethoven concerto, the greeting of a familiar voice, or birdsong on a still, spring morning. We feast with friends, savouring contrasting flavours and textures, appetites whetted by the aroma of simmering delicacies and brewing coffee. We're affirmed by the solid support of a friend's hug, or rest in the luxury of a hot bath, or are thrilled by the caress of a lover. Some of the deepest pleasures in life come from engaging and attending to our physical senses in response to the world around us.

There is, however, a great potency in these gifts, a potency that can overwhelm. Unbalanced pursuit of physical pleasure can destroy lives and relationships. Repeated overindulgence tends to reduce the delight while increasing the demand for more, trapping us in patterns of addiction that have lost all sense of celebration.

Fearing these dangers, groups and societies throughout history have often turned against the celebration of the physical senses, rather than encouraging and training the self-discipline, healthy limits and rhythms that allow sensory delight to be wholesomely sprinkled throughout our lives. I wish communities could demonstrate a mixture of accountability and grace, rather than fear and mistrust, in response to the pleasures of life. We can be people who learn to feast and fast with joy.

A rhythm of fasting is a necessary part of celebration. When we fast we remember that our enjoyment of the earth requires a context of balance, justice and open-handed generosity. We practise self-control to remind ourselves that our appetites, our laziness and our fear of suffering should not stand in the way when we are called to difficult tasks. We leave fields fallow for a season so that the soil remains life-giving over time. The courage and strength to withhold pleasure for a reason, to be able to delay gratification, can help enable the best kind of engagement and enjoyment.

But sacrifice for the sake of sacrifice seems to completely miss the point. A call to universally sacrificing entirely for the sake of others would also seem to miss the point—if one extends the logic, one gets a mass of people all suffering "for each other's sake" without anyone seeking joy, pleasure and fulfilment in the goodness of creation. It would seem to me that the function of fasting and sacrifice is primarily to ensure that, whenever possible, the invitation to joy and pleasure is available to as many as possible.

Gratitude

Gratitude is a central part of the practice of celebration that has two important aspects: the first is that we affirm what we've been given, what's been made available to us. We "bless" the gift and the giver by responding with thanks. Even when a gift is a mixed blessing, we take note of the goodness or even the potential goodness of what we have been given.

The second important aspect of gratitude is that it undermines the development of a sense of entitlement. Gratitude affirms that we have not demanded, we are not owed, that which we have been given. Those who feel entitled may find it very difficult to celebrate life. With the seasoning of gratitude absent, their intended delight may be flavourless.

Gratitude is not without its complications. Between people, practices of thanksgiving can get tangled up in social manners and obligations that create burdens instead of the joys of spontaneous thanks that are freely given and unexpectedly received.

Another complication arises as more and more people question or reject the notion of God. An inner sense of gratitude could become stifled by a sense of disconnection from the traditions and forms that used to give it expression. An agnostic farmer may be filled with awe in response to an especially abundant harvest, but to whom can he express his thanks? An atheist may be filled with wonder at the beauty of a mountain hike, recognizing the more-than-deserved health and resources that enable her to enjoy it, yet not know how to voice her appreciation.

Based on the human intuition from which gratitude springs (as well as the psychological affirmation of its benefits), I'm inclined to think that the act of expressing gratitude is more important than the theological or philosophical clarity that might guide it.

Celebrating the folk arts

When we think of how celebration is expressed in cultures around the world, the most typical examples are probably related to the dramatic folk arts: storytelling, music and dance. Here the celebration of beauty joins together with the remembering, the re-enactment, of key moments and movements in the lives of individuals and communities. Here, often, the integration of the mundane and the spiritual, the pragmatic and the imputation of meaning, takes place, and here the trajectory for the future—the vision of the gathered community—is embodied.

We might consider the dramatic telling of a legend explaining why some animals are hunted and not others. Or we could feel the jubilant energy of a barn dance after a full harvest had been gathered. A song might be sung about a remembered heroine, complete with victory and tragedy.

Western culture seems to be losing touch with the meaning and practice of these folk arts in the traditional sense. Partly this has been a result of the movement toward individualism and commercialism. Music and dance have divided rather than united the generations, often becoming overly sexualized and consumeristic. The traditional beauty and meaning of folk dances are pushed to the sidelines. Public storytelling has largely morphed into the private reading of books (for the shrinking minority who still read), and the art of film that has taken over is often reduced to a sensationalized "fast-food" version of story. The arts have such potential to draw us together into shared experiences. New creative conversations are waiting to be stimulated.

Even though we may now be getting our contemporary "folk arts" by way of private screens or earbuds, the recent emergence of "viral videos" and "memes"[1] are demonstrations of the urge to create shared culture. We feel left out around the proverbial water cooler if we haven't seen the latest social media craze. We want common experiences to enhance our interaction. It is unfortunate that many of these new versions of shared culture tend to be shallow and easily exploited.

Of course, those who can afford it still have a wide range of concerts and events to attend, and thrifty culture-watchers can probably find plenty of opportunities as well. Rich examples of the folk arts still exist. From the symphony orchestra to community theatre to a break-dance competition at a youth centre, people still gather to celebrate through the arts, making and expressing meaning as they do so.

We become what we celebrate

What we choose to celebrate is crucial because celebrating is one of the ways in which we declare our ideals, our recollection of the past and our vision for the future. Celebration helps orient us. If we commemorate the heroes of competitive economics, we help create an ongoing expectation of winners and losers. If we honour moments of reconciliation, we help our communities to keep imagining that enemies need not always be enemies.

Celebration is part of how we remember who we are and how we came to be. Nations tell the story of their origins in ways that often continue to shape their national character. In their Passover celebration, Jews keep alive the story of their liberation from slavery, reminding them to live with humble gratitude and encouraging them not to enslave or oppress others. Muslims observe Ramadan as the season when the Quran was revealed, reinforcing the importance of that teaching for their ongoing lives.

The central Christian celebration of the Eucharist or Communion is another, which clearly ties together past, present and future. The sacrament re-enacts the last supper of Jesus and his followers, especially recalling the centrality of love and service expressed in Jesus' willingness to die rather than lead a violent

---

[1] A piece of culture that is highly reproducible and spreads broadly and quickly, such as a poster on social media.

revolution. Simultaneously, the symbolic meal is considered a foretaste of the archetypal banquet table, the feast to which all are invited to share: outsiders and insiders, first and last. It is a sad irony, therefore, that so often in Christian history the celebration has been used to exclude rather than include.

I happen to be writing this on Remembrance Day—the day Canadians celebrate those who fought and died, particularly in the World Wars. As someone who grew up in a peace church tradition (Mennonite) dedicated to nonviolence, this day always has its awkward elements. There is no denying the courage and sacrifice of soldiers who fought for what they believed in, and the loss of their lives is certainly to be remembered. Yet, every time we celebrate the heroism of war, we lead many young people to envision their own heroism with a gun in their hand. When we commemorate a military victory, we tend to practise the denial of a history that shows time and again that the victors have been tainted by the same evil they sought to vanquish.

At the same time, most North Americans don't even know the story of how the European Union was formed, in spite of it being a development that has transformed a continent with a past of nearly constant warfare for thousands of years into a continent largely at peace. Most Europeans now could hardly imagine the possibility of fighting against a European neighbour. We need to get better at honouring moments of cooperation and reconciliation rather than the more dramatic but cyclical tales of military victory and defeat.

Celebrating upstream

If one of the purposes of celebrating is to draw attention to what we want to become, then we most need to celebrate that which is best but is not given attention in the society around us. In other words, we need to be very intentional about celebrating that which is countercultural in our communities. Taking note of efforts to paddle upstream, against the flow of society, encourages and makes possible a different way of being in the world.

This might mean celebrating environmental care or the beauty of simplicity and limits in the midst of a society that glorifies consumerism, greed and the unsustainable exploitation of the earth. It might mean celebrating inclusion of the marginalized in a culture that dehumanizes outcasts.

In many communities it would feel socially difficult for a family to buy most of its clothing from second-hand stores. We were fortunate to be a part of a community that celebrated such choices, enabling us to survive with a low income. There would have been incredible stress if we'd felt pressured to make regular trips to the mall to buy new clothes for the kids and ourselves. Similarly, choosing difficult environmental choices is hard when those choices are not honoured in a community. It's hard enough to overcome our own laziness, choosing to walk or take public transportation, but it's even harder when our friends and colleagues don't celebrate those choices with us.

Some groups have taken this to such extremes that they end up isolating themselves from the cultures around them. A long-standing example is the Amish, who have chosen to live in a largely farm-based society, rejecting much of the modern world. Their avoidance of prideful fashion and competitive worldliness can look exemplary, and their farming practices have been lauded by admirers such as Wendell Berry. Yet it's hard not to feel that something is lost when being separate is such a central part of how they live out their story. Even with a leaning toward celebrating upstream, we also need eyes that see all that is to be celebrated in the cultures in which we're immersed.

Celebration and competition

One of the paradoxes of celebration is its interaction with the notion of competition. Some see competition as a terrible thing—a practice deeply ingrained in the societies of the West that creates a sense of individualism and triggers struggles with self-esteem from early childhood onwards. Others see competition as the motivation toward greatness. We could even see within this tension the foundation of the battles between the systems of capitalism and socialism.

As with other paradoxes, we need to find our way into a healthy rhythm of competition that draws out its best aspects while protecting us from its worst. The dark face of competition is seen when victory over-against others comes to dominate the motivation. To lose, then, becomes crushing, and temptations toward envy and malice are not far away.

But competition need not be so dark. When the joy of competition comes from the love of the game and of the aesthetic heights toward which it reaches, something altogether different emerges. Now a competitive striving can become the motivation and energy that fuels excellence. Such competition can see a deep respect and even love emerge between opponents. All can be uplifted by the beauty that emerges out of such competition.

In communities that know how to keep competition focused on the joy of the game and the aesthetics of excellence (including, and perhaps especially, the "excellence" of fun), celebration can be energetically expressed in games and sports. It might even be possible to speculate that an outcome of enjoyment by all sides could be something of a test of a healthy spirit of competition in a community.

But this balance is about much more than sports and games. Unhealthy competition and our overworked tendency to compare ourselves with others get in the way of our ability to honour examples of living well. We become concerned with the envy created in those who feel they are left behind, but in the meantime our communities suffer because we have not often known how to motivate and energize one another to reach for the excellent and beautiful lives that we could be living. Perhaps we could find a better balance.

Self-forgetting

One of the most beautiful aspects of celebration comes during that moment when we naturally forget ourselves. We are so caught up in that with which we are deeply engaged that we are finally freed from our tedious self-centredness and self-consciousness. Yet it happens without putting ourselves down; we actually feel connected to what we are celebrating. Artists get lost in their work, religious folks in their worship, sports fans in the great comeback and music fans in the rock concert.

Ironically, it may even be in these moments that we feel most "inside of our own skins"—solid and centred. It's as if we were made to celebrate.

So, celebration is the practice of the joy of life. When celebration is inclusive and integrated with the other two responsive rhythms (lament and acceptance), it signals that we are responding well to life.

Getting Practical

Hold movie nights and book chats. The millions of people eager for every volume of Harry Potter demonstrate society's hunger for shared culture. People want to experience something that they know others are experiencing as well, and this can become the ground for rich, shared conversation. Movie nights and book chats provide opportunities for this kind of shared cultural conversation to take place about media offerings that are less universal. Powerful storytelling, well-shaped characters and evocative imagery in good books and film are potentially transformative, but we need to learn how to slow down our appreciation of these gifts and increase the rich dialogue they can generate.

Eat slow food. I am currently in the best small group I have ever been in. After decades of small groups (some great, some less so), my wife and I were nearly burned out from the leadership responsibilities that were so often expected. Taking time to imagine what we would be excited to do, we decided on an evening with a cluster of friends surrounding a table of carefully prepared food. And so, after slowly relaxing amid the food, wine and fellowship around the table, we let our conversation drift toward a stimulating or challenging book of spiritual interest that we have agreed to read.

Engage in community fasting and feasting. Encourage a group of people, perhaps an organization of some kind, to combine a fast and a feast. The feast can come before or after a fast (like the traditional pancake supper before lent or Easter dinner after) or they can be integrated (like the Muslim *iftar* suppers during Ramadan, beginning at sunset after a day of fasting). Find a way to make the fast filled with shared meaning. When the feast focuses on quality homemade or locally prepared food rather than something too uniquely "gourmet" or something overly processed, it can satisfy all palates and not alienate those with simpler tastes.

Honour people and their stories. Most of us are hungry for affirmation. Long term, consistent service is so often taken for granted. Beautiful moments of loving sacrifice are witnessed only by one or two. When we find ways to honour people and share their stories (or invite them to tell their stories), we do two beautiful things: we encourage those who may well need encouragement, and we inspire others as to what is possible. I think we often hesitate to honour people in our local communities because we have concerns that people may start doing things for the sake of attention, or that we'll hurt those we inevitably leave out. I suspect with some thoughtful creativity we could manage these risks.

2 LAMENTING

*The deeper that sorrow carves into your being,
the more joy you can contain.
Is not the cup that holds your wine the very cup
that was burned in the potter's oven?*

– Kahlil Gibran

*"Daddy it's ok when I'm sad
because the water in my eyes
makes the world sparkle!"*

– JoJo (a friend's three year old)

Imagine sitting in a concert of a talented folk singer as she mourns some personal loss in song. You wonder how it can feel so right for her to express such heartache, reminding all her listeners of their own. Or you walk out to a lonely beach with a friend whose child has recently died, and he shouts out his pain at the waves until he is hoarse. Or at home after a hard day's work, while watching the news and seeing one more tragic bombing of innocents, you inexplicably feel tears streaming down your face instead of becoming numb as you usually do.

~

Just picturing these things can make us ache because we all know that human lives are filled with moments of pain, suffering and loss. Even if our own experience has been relatively free of devastating events, we see it all around us. The rage, anguish, desolation and bitterness need to be expressed and shared. Lament is the active and intentional expression of our pain, sorrow and anger.

Lament is the twin of celebration. Without a matching rhythm of lament, celebration becomes false or shallow. Many have noticed over the centuries that fully experiencing joy requires that we also let ourselves experience times of sorrow, anger and deep pain. If we hold back on honest expression of these more difficult emotions, we will keep much of our emotional participation in happiness locked out as well. Facing and expressing what is going wrong keeps the potential for celebration to inflate and exhilarate grounded and humble.

One of the reasons that I am passionate about our need to lament is because of the one and only time that a dream was so meaningful for me that I felt it was a gift from God. My oldest daughter had been born three months premature and had lost her sight as a result; at the time of the dream she was seven. In spite of her blindness, she was growing and maturing well, and she, and we, were coping with the loss. The trying part was being a part of a particular Christian culture that had expectations that one should continually seek and expect that God might heal her. Enough of me believed this myself, or at least wondered about the possibility, that I was becoming incredibly frustrated, spiritually. My ability to relate honestly and deeply with God had been hindered for some time because of the anger and frustration that I felt toward God, but I continued to brush this aside. Intellectually, it didn't take all that much humility to be fairly sure that if God and I had different points of view, I was the one in the wrong. So, instead of lamenting and dealing honestly with my pain and anger, I continued to try to choose trust, assuming this was the right approach. But this left my body and emotions behind.

Then I had a dream that I was in a non-denominational megachurch that thrived on upbeat worship. Not only was I present, but I was up on stage, kicking up my heels with a chorus line of dancers backing up the worship band (only in a dream, I assure you). An enthusiastic worship leader kept the energy high and at one point called out to the celebrating congregation, "Who out there is happy? Who wants to praise God?" People responded with whoops and shouts and raised hands. Then as the song ended, almost as if he didn't really think about what he was doing, he said, "And now who out there is sad or angry?" At first there was no response, as the whole congregation was taken aback. Then slowly hands started going up all around the church. The emotional punch of that moment in the dream is something I still feel deep inside whenever I recall it. No one had a clue what to do—there was a sense of a thousand, suddenly honest worshippers realizing, "Now what? We don't have any songs for this." I woke up aware that I needed to find ways to express my own anger and frustration to God, and I also needed to become a promoter of lamentation in my counselling practice.

Though I didn't find many tools to help me do this at first, I chose to be more directly honest about my feelings and talked about them with others. I concluded that my penchant for playing sad piano music by Beethoven and Chopin was the only way I gave myself permission for sad feelings. I paid new attention to examples of lament in literature, film and song. I sought out the psalms of lament, among the few remaining connections I had to a time when culture gave a lot more consideration to our need to express frustration and loss. For my own sake as well as that of my clients, I paraphrased some and joined in the cry of "How long?"

Learning from the ancients

Over a third of the Psalms (sometimes called the prayer book or hymn book of Second Temple Judaism, the Jewish faith of the centuries before Christ) are lament psalms—some expressing the lament of an individual and some the lament of a people. In both cases, we see that one of the values of this kind of expressive poetry is that it provides a form for the experience of pain and suffering. Practical theologian John Swinton writes in *Raging with Compassion*,

> ... it becomes clear that the psalms of lament are not designed simply to express human pain and suffering. They are also designed to form human pain and suffering in quite specific ways. The psalms of lament provide a language and a structure within which pain, suffering, grief and despair can be ritualized and worshippers moved from one way of seeing their situation to a radically different way of seeing.

What the form teaches us is that lament is a rhythm, a passage. Lamenting is not wallowing or drowning in a sea of pain—it is expressing the suffering in a way that helps to keep us from getting stuck or lost in it. As a friend of mine recently wrote, "We name the desolation of winter, while hoping for the coming of spring."[2] A lament is an act of faith—even when the pain expressed is the pain of doubt and despair, it is addressed to the One with whom we are longing to reconnect, or even if the complaint can find no listening ears there is the declaration that it is still worth crying out. There is trust that what we have been experiencing is not the way things should be.

The form of the psalms continues by leading those who lament to recall past experiences—the bigger picture. There is the confident assertion that the experienced injustice, or the absence of God, is not fitting with the character of God or the universe God created. Recalling this in the act of lament leads from a legitimate complaint to a hope-filled cry for mercy and deliverance. There is growing trust that there will be a response. Those who lament wait and listen.

I have talked to many people who have doubted the existence of God in response to seeing great tragedies in the world or

---

[2] Ashley Burtch, http://www.hamiltoncommons.ca/cry-for-hope/

suffering in their own lives. Who can blame them? I wonder, though, whether it is not so much the absence of a philosophically reasonable justification of God that leads people to doubt as it is the lack of knowing how to cry out our pain. Is it really our intellect that struggles? After all, plenty of reasonable theories of theodicy—explanations for how a God could allow evil to happen—exist, but they are usually emotionally unsatisfying. I wonder if our emotional need isn't to pound our fists on the chest of a God big enough to take it.

The psalms of lament show us that it's okay to do this, and give us examples to guide us into lamenting. Some psalms (e.g. 88) end without response. Sometimes the waiting and listening following lament are filled with silence. In the book of Job, we read the story of a man who ranted for a long time before he received a rather overwhelming response. Even then God answered none of the charges and questions that Job had raised. Lament is not a quick self-help cure or a guarantee of any particular response, but it does have the potential to clear our head and still our soul so that we can reconnect with life in spite of our pain.

How far can lament go?

Whether recalling the Balkans in the nineties or following the news in the border territories of central Africa today, we can hardly help but be overwhelmed by a mixture of feelings in response to the systematic rape, torture and butchering of innocent victims. We know that the longing for revenge after such acts is only natural among the survivors. Does our hearing of such horrors at a great distance, together with the smaller frustrations and injustices we experience directly, make us seek outlets in forms such as revenge movies? We see the evil perpetrators do worse and worse things, until our hatred is finally purged by the cathartic violent revenge that destroys the dehumanized villains. Lacking a more articulate release for our feelings, are these films really the best outlet we can find? They may not be good for us, but they certainly are popular and understandable.

While they make many contemporary readers uncomfortable, the ancient laments expressed these desires more directly. The psalms did not hold back when those suffering injustice cried out in response. From the relatively mild:

> O that you would kill the wicked, O God,
>   and that the bloodthirsty would depart from me (Ps. 139.19)

to the really troubling:

> O daughter Babylon, you devastator!
>   Happy shall they be who pay you back
>   what you have done to us!
> Happy shall they be who take your little ones
>   and dash them against the rock! (Ps. 137. 8–9)

These psalms demonstrate the community's acknowledgement that after being on the receiving end of horrific violence and injustice, we must give voice to the depth of pain and longing for vengeance that arise in our souls. If these intensely felt reactions cannot be expressed, they will wreak havoc when suppressed, either deadening the soul or leaking out in all kinds of inappropriate hostility and bitterness.

Yet research has made it clear that catharsis alone does not cleanse a person of pent-up anger. If our feelings, perceptions and attitudes are not changed through or after such cathartic lament, we may even risk making our anger worse. Perhaps for a short time, this may be a better result than sinking into lifeless depression. But the hope for healing and renewal is that the honest facing of deep grief can permit the possibility of forgiveness before retribution is sought and the cycle of violence continues. The "cursing" psalms are not an encouragement to wish for or even to take revenge; they are an acceptance of the reality that powerful desires for retribution need to be given voice before they are transformed and released.

Alone and together

There are many more ordinary ways to express our pain than following the poetry of the Psalms. Music, visual art, or vigorous exercise can all be a part of the process of lamenting. And perhaps one of the most common of all ways is to cry on the shoulder of a trustworthy listener.

The social aspect of lament can be more complicated than it was for celebration. What if no one wants to hear your lament? What if you are afraid that expressing your pain will make you feel judged? What if your family or even your larger culture haven't provided you with any tools even to begin trying to lament?

Sometimes it will seem right to make our complaint on our own. In silence, out loud, or writing in a journal, we find some way to express what is wrong. But sometimes this will not be enough. Sometimes we need others to lament with us, or at least to serve as an audience for our cries.

Not everyone will be able to do this for us. Many people are uncomfortable with emotions, especially the messier ones, and lament can certainly be messy. We should try not to be discouraged if an attempt at sharing our pain with a friend feels stifled by a quick reassurance or even blatant rejection of our feelings. Such an experience doesn't mean our lamenting was wrong; it just means our audience wasn't ready. If we can't find someone among our friends and acquaintances that we trust, we may need to seek an experienced professional or pastoral counsellor.

When a community laments together, there is an important public acknowledgement that there is brokenness around us. It is the opposite of burying our heads in the sand and lets the most direct victims of tragedy know that others stand in solidarity with them. Public lament also models for those who are hesitant that it is okay to express our pain. We can all join in the protest with full voice. We see the importance of public outcry when there is a terrorist attack or when a troubled teen commits suicide in response to bullying.

Finally, public lament can be an energizing initiator of public action. Since the expressions of pain are in the public arena, there can be a re-orienting of unfair, ignorant or bigoted responses. Especially at first, we often hear of knee-jerk reactions to shared tragedies that are stereotyped and generalized; public conversation at least has the potential to let the anger be channelled in more productive directions. Then organized responses can start working toward community and political change, motivated by the shared conviction that something is, indeed, wrong with the way things are.

Overcoming denial

When we see the laments of those around us—when we realize that others are openly facing and feeling their pain and admitting that parts of life can be really terrible—we are invited to break through our own denial. The world is not by any means a consistently pretty place. This must be expressed and felt.

Even when there is a background of peaceful and comfortable circumstances, people can be overwhelmed when death suddenly comes in clusters. A parent dies, and then in the months that follow an aunt on one side of the family dies and a young cousin we often played with as kids succumbs to cancer. All of a sudden, after a decade or two of being relatively untouched by death, we seem overcome because it seems there is so much death in the world. We may not be prepared for this kind of experience partly as a result of our denying the persistent normality of death.

We hear countless testimonies of how truly facing death, staring its immanence in the face, can be an important, life-enhancing challenge. Knowing that our own time is limited and knowing that the time we have with loved ones may be briefer than we wish helps empower us to "seize the day." But our denial of death is solid and thick, and it will take more than occasional intentionality to break through. Facing and lamenting the countless smaller losses of our lives helps us chip away at our denial of death. We are then a little more prepared when accident or illness suddenly dismantles the rest of the wall.

Perhaps harder than facing the reality of death is facing the horror of human evil. On the one hand denying this reality might seem impossible since we hear of these things on the news more and more. However, this demonstrates that denial is not breached by the quantity of communicated facts. We are, in fact, increasingly numbed by the sheer volume of this kind of news, if we still bother to look. This is why we need to practise lament more than ever. To be inundated with constant tales of horror without a shared opportunity to voice the emotional pain of what is taking place is to become hardened and emotionally cut off. Personally, I find that the right kind of movie at the right time can really help with this, though my preference is for those films that humanize the enemies around us, reminding us that we're all hurting, rather than the films that tempt us with the quick satisfaction of revenge.

There is a real emotional danger of becoming overwhelmed by the suffering of others. So if we are keeping ourselves alive and vulnerable by feeling and expressing the pain of seeing the misery and tragedy around us, we may need to limit how much we expose ourselves to all the horrors that exist in the world. This is, after all, another rhythm, not something we want to get lost in. Just as healthy grief is a season, rather than a bottomless pit, so lament is a passage that we journey through in order to stay grounded, honest and humble as we return to moments of celebration and acceptance.

The opposite of healthy lament – wallowing

There are unhelpful imitations of lamenting. After two decades as a professional counsellor, I've come to see wallowing as one of the unhealthiest mental practices. Lots of people can relate to the familiarity of thoughts getting trapped in unhelpful loops that play over and over in one's head. Wallowing doesn't lead anywhere; it's the expression of those who, at least at some level, want to stay with the familiarity of their pain.

Perhaps the worst form of wallowing is self-pity. Usually this involves taking a mixture of real and perceived victimization and ensuring that it lasts. Of course, this is not the conscious intention. But if we keep looking, we can always find evidence to convince ourselves that we are especially mistreated by others or by life. Once this kind of wallowing becomes habitual, it begins to pervade one's nonverbals and conversations with others. Since self-pity is one of the most socially noxious attitudes, wallowers increasingly slip into isolation and unsatisfying relationships (often as acquaintances but never as close friends). This, in turn, reinforces the self-pity, and the wallowing becomes quicksand. Wallowers often come for help and a listening ear, gladly sharing their troubles and perhaps even fruitfully accepting help in an immediate situation. Yet, very rarely will they admit and seek help for their long-time habit of wallowing, which is at the root of their difficulties with life. Kind and intentional people will occasionally confront this pattern in a friend, when they see it, out of love—sometimes with success.

Others wallow in their self-righteous anger. We might rather call this stewing. Their anger is always simmering beneath the surface. Particularly among those with whom they live, this anger becomes regularly visible in subtle or not-so-subtle ways. They feel constantly frustrated by others or themselves, seeing the world as unfair. Typically, they feel entitled to things that are beyond their grasp. Except for the most problematic (who may eventually be jailed or sent to anger-management courses), these folks may know their limits—not healthy limits, but those that preserve the status quo. So they tone their anger down before they lose their jobs or ease up on their families before their spouses walk out. Those who stew in anger are less likely to seek help on their own, but might eventually be forced in that direction. Ironically, once it comes to that, those who stew in self-righteous anger may actually be more open to change than those sadly wallowing in self-pity. Anger is more energizing than self-pity.

A third kind of wallowing is that of being mired in general negativity. Occasionally I've heard this referred to as wearing "shit-coloured glasses." In some ways, these can be the least stuck of the three. For some people, this negativity feeds depression and hopelessness, but other people seem to be able to live well and are barely aware of how negative their views are on everything. Of course, the more it leads to depression, the more it is debilitating. While general negativity might seem as socially unpleasant as self-pity, this is not quite the case because this kind of negativity more easily draws others into it: everyone pounces together on a common enemy. Typical gossip, of course, can be a form of this.

For those who struggle with depression, getting out of this pit of negativity is both more difficult and more important. I believe the best pathway—like swimming sideways instead of fighting against a rip tide—is not to argue with oneself but to give attention to something neutral and sensory, like the "walk into peace" exercise mentioned earlier. This creates space in which one can choose to follow a more positive direction.

Those without depressive tendencies will have fewer motivations to get out of this pit and may barely experience it as a pit at all. Gaining awareness of the effect that this negativity can have on others and on entire communities might help these folks to choose to commit to trying to break what is largely a bad social habit. Those who succeed may even find that there are some unexpected personal gains to be found when avoiding the trap of negativity.

What all of these poor imitations of lamenting have in common is that the ranges of thinking and feeling have become narrowed. We get stuck when we have lost touch with the rhythms that keep our lives growing and that enable our maturing in spite of the difficulties of life. There also seems to be evidence that consistent negative activity hogs the brain's resources, shutting down more constructive mental activities like problem solving, perspective shifting and the understandings gained through clarifying experience in language. The form that is provided through lamenting, as opposed to grumbling and wallowing, has the potential of changing this pattern. The fuller, more honest expression of pain leads out of the endless "stuckness" into listening, hoping and waiting—especially when combined with some of the practices of the next section on acceptance.

Lamenting is a necessary part of a life of authenticity. We need to lament in order to live honestly even with ourselves and our bodies, which will usually be affected by our pain and maybe especially the pain that we might otherwise deny. Lament is the struggle to articulate and get through a season of pain, as opposed to staying lost or mired within it.

Getting Practical

Share highs and lows. A simple way to incorporate a balance of celebrating and lamenting in daily life is the practice of sharing "highs and lows." For many years, we have made this a part of life in our household. With long- or short-term guests, this adds a wonderful quality to the conversation around the table. While this can be as simple as briefly sharing the best or worst moments of our days, we learned our practice from the Ignatian contemplative tradition, which uses what they call the *Examen* as a regular discipline of reflecting on the presence of God in all aspects of our everyday lives. Our simplified version has been to light a candle to symbolize inviting the presence of God into the midst of the activity. Then anyone who wishes shares two parts of the day: one part that has been life enhancing and one that has felt draining.

Listen to the pain of others. We can make it more difficult for others to lament when we express discomfort with it. Notice what happens inside you when others express pain, hurt or anger. Many of us have little tolerance for this. Some of us dismiss those who speak their pain, while others, too quickly, offer glib reassurance or deny that there is any real reason for the suffering. Consider how you can honour the need for others to lament and model acceptance of their emotion. Perhaps your listening can transform another's unhelpful wallowing into healthy lament. Or you may later need to lament yourself, in order to unload after the negativity you have picked up from listening.

Embody a lament. Laments are often needed by our bodies as well as our minds. Laments that are just a brief acknowledgement in our mind that we are angry or sad are weak laments. If you find a poem or song that fits, read it aloud, or share your lament with a friend. Or say words of lament, aloud or quietly, while doing a vigorous physical activity. Or try some of the expressively embodied examples that have been mentioned—play sad or angry music, express your pain in art or dance, or shout at the top of a mountain, on a lonely beach or in an empty field.

Pray the Psalms. Praying the words of a psalm can remind us of the fullness of expression that has been often missing from our own more tempered and emotionless prayers. Try to enter into various psalms as expressions—when grateful, voice the exuberant praise of a psalm like 100. And when you recognize that you're in the midst of pain and anguish, cry out with the psalmist with psalms like 6 or 13.

Write a lament. Sometimes the words of others simply don't quite fit or express your own suffering. Try writing out your own lament in poetry or prose. If you are familiar with the Psalms, you can use the form of a lament psalm as a template. State your complaint and the way you feel about it; then write out whatever you hear or feel in response after the complaint. Can you find any words of hope or trust in your heart?

3 ACCEPTING

*...All shall be well, and all shall be well,
and all manner of thing shall be well*

– Julian of Norwich

*The most fundamental aggression to ourselves, the
most fundamental harm we can do to ourselves, is
to remain ignorant by not having the courage
and the respect to look at ourselves
honestly and gently.*

– Pema Chödrön

In quietness and in trust shall be your strength

– The prophet Isaiah

Imagine a successful businessman whose family life is in shambles because of his drinking and his workaholic life. Alienated from his children and forced to see the truth when his wife leaves him, he faces the painful reality of his life, steps up to the microphone at an AA meeting, and admits that he is an alcoholic. The last months of his life have been a little like hell and a surface optimism has been burned away, but in quieter moments—which he now allows himself—he notices that an inner nagging voice of self-hatred is gone.

Or imagine a middle-aged woman visiting her perpetually critical mother, who greets her at the door by saying, "Oh, I guess the diet isn't working?" In the past this would have set off explosions of anger and shame in her head, but recently she's been letting herself see her mom's brokenness, social insecurities, and the generational pattern of criticism that her mom fell into. As a result, the daughter chooses to forgive her mom and herself. Instead of her old sarcasm, she simply hugs her mom and says, "I'm not really on a diet, Mom."

~

In contrast to the highs and lows of celebration and lament, acceptance represents a response of quiet contentment and trust-filled awareness of present reality. Often we need to surrender—to let go of the anxious grasping for control that resists this sweet rest. When we find the ability to do so, we come to realize that the joy of this acceptance can be as powerful as the joy of celebration, being closely related to the rhythms of both celebration and lament.

Acceptance is simultaneously simple and challenging. In part this is because what is needed is often deep assent to something that doesn't seem to require our assent. Yet we resist. Why should we be asked to accept the past when we clearly have no power over what already happened? Why is it so hard to accept our parents, when we have no choice over who they are and no ability to change their personalities? Why is it so hard to accept our limitations and weaknesses, when we've never met anyone who was perfect?

This paradoxical element means that we can't accomplish acceptance by effort and exertion. There is nothing to push on. In fact, it is the whole notion of pushing that we are being asked to give up. We have to relax into acceptance; we have to stop pushing and simply be where we are. When we can take a deep breath and believe that, at least for now, it is actually okay to be where we are, we know we are beginning to practise acceptance.

At the heart of the rhythm of acceptance is the art of contemplation or meditation, the practice of becoming aware of ourselves and our surroundings, of seeing and perceiving with honesty and compassion. When this practice is combined with an emerging belief or trust that all demands can be relinquished, that all expectations can be held loosely in an open palm, that deeply, fundamentally, everything is okay as it is—then the clarity of the vision that arises is flavoured with peace.

Stillness and silence

There are various ways to approach stillness. We can choose stillness by taking a walk along a quiet stream until the only thing we hear is the water tumbling over rocks or the occasional birdsong. We can be forced into stillness by a sudden disease or accident that leaves us unable to work. Some are able to find stillness riding on a crowded subway; some can't get still even while lying on a sunny beach.

There is a strange paradox in contemporary Western society: nearly everyone feels too busy too much of the time, and yet we spend an incredible amount of time browsing social media or watching television. It seems that we are running from stillness. Even those of us trying to be intentional about stillness and silence often encounter an inner anxiety as we approach stillness that makes us flee back to activity, or at least entertainment.

I suspect that there are no satisfying explanations for why so many of us feel that anxiety or resistance that make it difficult for us to get still. Rather than finding clear answers, I have found it more fruitful to learn ways to get around or push through the resistance. For me, there is no question that the most helpful practice through the years has been contemplative reading.

When I read certain books, I am fairly certain that something significant is taking place in my brain that allows a different way of thinking. Some of the typical "busy" thinking that tends to get in the way seems to stop or at least drift far into the background. I enter a "zone" in which I become far more intuitive. New insights arise; pieces seem to fall into place. I find something starting to make sense that I hadn't even realized I was troubled by. I like to think of this as prayer because I don't feel like I am doing this alone.

I say "certain books" but occasionally it might be anything: a news article, a book on psychology, a thoughtful email. But my more reliable companions during such moments of reading-induced stillness are authors like Thomas Merton, Wendell Berry, Richard Rohr, Simone Weil, Annie Dillard, Howard Thurman—authors who model contemplative wisdom. It's as though their words take me by the hand and lead me beside the still waters with which they have become familiar.

Getting outdoors is another path to stillness. When I am walking, I force myself to stop thinking and pay attention to what is around me. Climate change has brought cardinals with their unique whistling song to my small town. Since it's so fascinating to see these bright and beautiful birds, their song always gets my attention, and I start looking around. I escape my own repetitive or anxious thoughts. I look at the trees, the squirrels, and see which flowers are blooming this week. And as I do this I feel the stillness and peace growing stronger.

Music helps when I actually stop doing other things and listen to it. Giving my attention to classical music or thoughtful singer/songwriters can help bring me to a place of stillness. I've often been surprised at how new, "unstuck," thoughts about normal life enter my mind while listening intentionally to music. I might become aware of an emotion that has been present without my noticing for some time.

Perhaps oddly, what usually doesn't work for me is trying to sit silently and become still. I know this works well for some people, but during such times, my thoughts race here and there quite unproductively. I might, or might not, get somewhere if I focus my thoughts on a certain task. I suspect I haven't yet learned the patience to get beyond these initial difficulties.

I believe the common element to these ways of finding stillness is the enabling of whole-brained attention, the balanced availability of the left and right hemispheres of the brain. In my opening chapter I mentioned some of the ways in which these hemispheres operate differently. For me it is left-brained busyness that usually clogs up my attention. This works fine for specific problem solving, but lacks the open-minded awareness characteristic of the right hemisphere. My wife, on the other hand, seeks stillness with math puzzles like Sudoku or Ken-kens. I believe that for her, this stills a more right-brained busyness in her thinking by stimulating some left-brained clarity.

The key is that the paths are diverse, and we need to experiment to find our own way to stillness.

Seeing with compassion

For this attention and awareness to lead positively to acceptance, there needs to be an undergirding foundation of compassion. Seeing with judgment and condemnation won't lead anyone to peace and acceptance. Yet many of us have been well schooled in such harsh ways of seeing, and the habit can be hard to break.

One of the gifts of humanistic psychology has been the emphasis on listening and "unconditional positive regard" that were emphasized by psychotherapist, Carl Rogers. These days it is hard to realize that before the popularity of Rogers' views, therapists were not necessarily attempting to be warm and accepting. One of the most encouraging discoveries in my early years of counselling practice was that choosing unconditional positive regard worked. As a result of my own personality, I was as capable of being critical and negative about others (or myself) as the average person, but now I was expected to be warm and compassionate to whoever walked into my office. And it worked! By choosing to genuinely care and really pay attention to people, sincere compassion inevitably grew.

In "real life" this is not so inevitable. The intentionality and accountability of the therapy office are missing, as are the appropriate boundaries that limit how much a client's life will encroach on a therapist. But the principle still works. Compassion for ourselves and others can be a choice, though we are likely to need help. Many people have turned to their faith tradition to provide this help.

While the example of many churches may make this hard to believe, one of the central hallmarks of Jesus' teaching was the invitation to a judgment-free compassion. His ministry of healing, of welcoming the outcasts, and of teaching love for enemies demonstrated that his life revolved around compassion. Based on this, a traditional contemplative practice that has helped countless Christians learn to see more compassionately has been called "practising the presence of God."

In the 17th century, Brother Lawrence, a lay member of a Carmelite monastery wrote a small devotional book called *The Practice of the Presence of God*. At the heart of this brief volume was the basic skill of imaginatively practising the awareness that God was lovingly present in the midst of all the "common business" of one's life. By doing one's routine work out of submission to that loving presence, all this mundane work was transformed into prayer. And one of the key aspects of this transformation was a more compassionate attitude toward others and oneself.

This practice can become especially potent when this form of imaginative prayer is applied to inner healing for deep hurts. My doctoral work was focused on a narrative perspective on this inner healing, and I studied the phenomenon that sprung up in many pockets of the Christian church in the second half of the 20th century. Sometimes referred to as the "healing of memories," the core of this practice was to combine a vivid recollection of a wounding experience with the imaginative openness to the presence of God or the Spirit of Christ. Time after time, I have seen people begin to perceive the times of brokenness in their lives with new eyes as a result of this practice. By experiencing God as being lovingly present, even in the midst of a painful time, fresh ways of seeing and interpreting the meaning of an event were enabled. In most cases, this inner healing was transformative, shifting the way in which the wounding memory affected their present lives and emotions. What used to cause intense shame, guilt, fear, or bitterness would now be a reminder of grace and forgiveness.

Buddhist teachings on mindfulness and meditation have also taught many to learn to see themselves and others more compassionately. As in other Eastern beliefs, the emphasis is less on a sense of a personal divine presence and more on the interconnectedness of all life and spirit. The expected presence of suffering and hardship that Buddhism teaches makes it more natural to accept the pain that compassion sometimes requires.

Only when our awareness of self and others becomes deeply compassionate can we begin to face reality with honesty. Without compassion, we will always struggle to accept what is real because the truth about ourselves will be too painful and the truth about others might make us bitter and hostile. With compassion, we see the nuances beyond the black and white. We are open to empathy and context. We become willing to forgive, letting go of demands for others to fix what is not fixable.

Honesty and integrity

Self-deception is nearly universal, and we all have to learn to overcome it. Seeing with compassion enables us to start to imagine that it is truly okay to be a flawed human being. We are weak, broken, limited, and self-centred beings that are somehow still worthy of being treated with kindness, of being seen with delight.

Once we trust that this is really the case, we can start laying down our defences, admitting our mistakes, sharing our moments of shame, and seeing ourselves as we are. The Greek word *homologeo*, which usually translates as "confess" speaks to this. Etymologically it means "speaking the same as" or "agreeing." We speak the single-minded truth about ourselves and what we've done. It is the literal opposite of the "doublespeak" that is characteristic when we are deceiving ourselves and others.

The Catholic practice of the confessional is meant to invite parishioners into exactly this kind of honest accounting of oneself. The compassion of God is represented by the priest who invites this truth-telling and responds with absolution: the declaration of forgiveness and acceptance. Some of us might have concerns about the hierarchical power that can get tangled up in this practice, and many who have grown up in a Catholic tradition have learned to sidestep honesty by learning from their young peers to routinely confess the most typical and least stigmatizing sin they can think of. But behind the real and perceived obstacles, the ritual offers much potential. A lot fewer professional counsellors would be needed if we all had access to caring listeners who would hear our vulnerable confessions, responding with a grace and wisdom that confidently proclaimed, in spite of whatever was admitted, that we were okay, acceptable in the eyes of God and at least one other human being.

Confession thus has the ability to integrate the divided parts of ourselves. In other words, it leads to integrity. There is nothing wrong with recognizing that we are not entirely one, unified self. Wise interpreters of the human soul have always seen that there is a community of selves inside each of us. This does not mean that we have dissociative identity disorder (what used to be known as multiple personality disorder—the defining characteristic of which is that these personalities are entirely cut off from each other). It simply means that we have different parts of ourselves that affect us differently at various times and in contrasting ways. An angry self might emerge when we drink more than we should, or a silly, bubbly self takes over at a social event. A person who appears to all as meek and submissive may have internal fantasies that are violent. Which is the true self?

Integrity is not about flattening all of this diversity into one consistent self, but it does involve a weaving together of these selves so that they can all get along and work together. Just like a healthy community respects and accepts all of its members, the integrated self is honest about all its parts, including the shadow selves that think, feel, and perhaps even do things of which we aren't very proud. Accepting this inner diversity allows us to care for the unique needs of these shadow selves, addressing the insecurities, hurts or fears that may be fuelling the dark thoughts or actions. Without honest confession, these disowned parts of ourselves continue to do their damage in hidden corners of our being, and many relationships are broken as a result.

Forgiveness: Letting go of debts and record-keeping
Honesty has a reciprocal relationship with the practice of forgiveness (the giving up of debts and, at best, abandonment of the whole notion of keeping track). One of the most unique gifts of the Christian tradition is the depth and clarity of its teaching on forgiveness. At its root is Jesus' bold declaration that God was offering forgiveness as eagerly as the rejected father who ran out to welcome the "prodigal son." While the experience of forgiveness may require and, hence, follow the difficult step of confession, it is the forgiveness already offered that in most cases makes confession possible. How many could confess with true honesty and vulnerability if they expected condemnation and rejection as a result?

So forgiveness and honesty deepen each other as they go hand in hand. If my forgiveness of someone who wounds me is to be healthy, I will honestly name the wound and the actions that hurt me. This is not done in order to blame or cause further pain but to make possible an ongoing relationship based on honesty and understanding. Without this clear naming, the practice is not forgiveness but denial or minimizing. When accompanied by forgiveness, the clarity of spoken truth allows the one who has done wrong to be freed of the burden that has knowingly or unknowingly been carried. The way is cleared to begin negotiating what level of trust is or isn't possible, since there is also the honest recognition that deeply ingrained patterns of hurtful actions may be hard to change.

Forgiving ourselves adds another challenging step made possible by honesty. We may resist this very strongly if we are having trouble with integrity. The intensity of our desire not to "own" the weak and broken self that has made mistakes struggles against this clearing of the books. In order for us to forgive ourselves, we have to come to peace with the unchangeable reality that we do not live up to our ideals. We have to trust that self-condemnation is not the effective jailer that will keep our shadow selves from messing up in the future. Our best hope, rather, comes from compassionately welcoming our broken parts into the light where healing may lessen future mistakes.

Without forgiveness, an honest accounting of our wrongdoings and those of others is crushing, leading us toward a bitterness that saps the warmth and joy out of life. Relationships that survive in spite of unforgiveness will often slowly wither, lacking any intimacy. Alternatively, as forgiveness becomes a way of life, we can quit keeping records of wrongdoing altogether. The freedom that grows out of this acceptance of self and others enables engaged and committed relationships in spite of the messiness of living life together.

This does not mean, however, that we should rush or oversimplify the process of forgiveness. Research has shown that forgiveness that intentionally takes longer has a deeper effect on people. Rushed forgiveness may be incomplete or may cause a rift in our souls because part of ourselves can't let go of the hurt that quickly. When I counsel those who struggle with forgiveness, I invite people to do two things: commit themselves to a pathway of forgiveness and take the time they need to walk through that process fully and honestly.

Accepting weakness and limits

It seems that contemporary society is increasingly trying to pretend that we do not need to be constrained by limits. Recent political battles about climate change can be seen as the tension between those who accept the earth's limits and those who don't. Technology is often seen as the source of our supposed ability to overcome any apparent limits, and certainly some limits have been surpassed. But we might wonder how often even these apparent victories have costs that are still to be determined.

There is an ancient awareness of this tension with limits, seen in the mythical stories of Prometheus and Icarus. Prometheus, a trickster who had previously fooled Zeus into accepting inedible sacrifices, is punished for stealing fire from the gods for human use. His punishment is having his liver eaten out daily by an eagle (the liver being regenerated every night). Icarus uses technology—wings made of wax and feathers—created by his father, Daedelus, to fly out of his labyrinthine prison but is warned not to fly too near the sun. In his ambition or enthusiasm, he ignores this and approaches close enough to melt the wax which sends him crashing into the sea. Throughout history, these myths have elicited a mixed response. We want to celebrate at least aspects of the visionary and creative attempt to achieve the impossible, but we recognize the hubris that leads to inevitable tragedy.

In recent decades, we have become so enamoured with technology that we are increasingly tempted to imagine that Icarus could have soared to whatever heights he wanted with a few more years of research and development. We forget that hubris is still one of humanity's most tragic flaws, and no science or technology will transform hubris into a strength.

True hope lies in the acceptance of limits and in harmonizing our lives with the ecologies and economies that pay attention to those limits. We approach the miraculous when with creativity, courage, and joy we are fully integrated with the limits of our environment, our neighbours, and ourselves.

Accepting emotions

Our own limitations may be the hardest to accept. We come across them in our bodies, our personalities, our motivations and will. But one way that we experience these limits most directly is through our emotions.

Emotions are felt responses and reactions to the way in which we experience and perceive events. The way we consciously interact with our emotions is complex. Generally, we are not directly in charge of what we feel. Emotions are more like thermometer readings which enable us to get an indication of how we are perceiving things—giving us clues as to what events and observations mean to us both consciously and unconsciously.

We often respond very badly to our own emotions. We hate ourselves for being angry because we have been taught that anger is wrong or because we have seen the suffering that anger can create. So we suppress the anger instead of finding healthy ways to face it and express it. Or we have trained ourselves in self-pity so that our sadness and losses cascade—when we feel one sadness all our losses are revisited—and we feel on the brink of being lost in a deep pool of despair.

Shame and fear are perhaps the emotions that make us most aware of our limitations and weakness, and thus we hate them most of all. When we experience trauma, these are the emotions most likely to overwhelm us to the point of "blowing a fuse," shutting down our normal ways of processing and making sense of what happened. Our minds, not given a chance to digest and integrate what has happened, are left with lasting emotional wounds like PTSD (post-traumatic stress disorder).

Fear surrounds our lives in so many ways. We are afraid of threats to our physical, relational and spiritual security. Courage is so crucial to our actions and choices, for ourselves, our families and our communities, that societies have often tried to force it on us by socially labelling cowardice as one of the greatest weaknesses. Unfortunately, we often misinterpret the experience of feeling fear with that of being a coward. Wise people have often reminded us that courage is not the absence of fear, but the determination to choose the wise and compassionate course of action in the face of fear. And even while doing our best to grow in courage, we need to be compassionate about those frequent lapses when fear makes us weak.

It is hard for me to admit the extent of fear still present in my life. I have managed to make some sacrificial choices in my life, but usually these have been strategically chosen to risk the lesser fears I find tolerable (such as choosing limited financial security) and avoiding those that run deep (such as living in the midst of regions with random, senseless violence). I can admire the courage of those who choose to be a compassionate presence in the midst of that kind of violence, but the dark side of that admiration can be a shame about my own fears. Will that shame help grow my courage for when it's needed? Not likely. Better to honestly face our fears whenever we encounter them, and try to practise taking small steps of courage whenever we see a worthwhile opportunity. If we fail the test, we accept that we all have a diversity of gifts, and outstanding courage may not be ours. Or perhaps our courage in one area of life balances our lack of courage elsewhere.

Even more at the heart of our weakness is the feeling of shame itself. We could even say that shame is the emotion we feel when we are confronted by perceived inadequacies, especially when those inadequacies are exposed in front of others. Many times this may be a false shame, caused, for example, by something that someone else has done to us or by misperceived flaws. At other times, shame accurately reflects that we have been caught—either by our own awareness or by others—in behaviour that is truly shameful or just typical human weakness.

In either case, hope does not come from running and hiding, much as we are tempted. We overcome shame when we choose honest vulnerability, trusting that all humanity shares our frailty and that our relationships will grow best through open communication. At best, we have the opportunity of being affirmed in a loving and trusting relationship, experiencing that we are accepted in spite of our real or perceived flaws. Empowered by this acceptance and security, we can acknowledge and turn from truly shameful behaviours, redeeming the experience of shame, where truly necessary, through a changed life. But we need to choose people who have come to terms with their own shame if we want listeners that we can trust with our vulnerability.

As we learn to accept our emotions and the weaknesses from which they spring, we can increasingly choose curiosity and compassion as the welcoming committee for these feelings. When we become aware of a strong or unexpected emotion, we begin by acknowledging it and allowing it to have a place: "For a time, Frustration, you can stay. Sit here at the table while I ask you some questions and figure out why you've come."

Curiosity is a much more helpful reaction to our emotions than variations of rejection or self-blame. Since emotions reveal something about our perceptions and interpretations, we can wonder why they've come. Possibly, or possibly not, emotions tell us something reliable about what is happening around us.

We can then choose to consider what the emotions are telling us and what actions we want to choose. For example, one evening I might notice that I am feeling down and without energy. Giving attention to this awareness, I suspect that this is because something I had looked forward to earlier in the day fell through. Recognizing the disappointment, I honour that this makes sense given what happened. However, since there is no longer anything to be done about it (unless perhaps the disappointment is deep enough that I need to lament or express it aloud to someone), I realize that I don't want my evening plans to fall through because of my mood. Acknowledging and understanding my feelings (and perhaps consciously "holding them" for a moment or expressing them) increases my ability to then choose to shift my focus to what is ahead. If I don't honour them with that brief curiosity, the feelings may continue to try to get my attention all evening long.

Obviously, many feelings run deeper than this example or involve more complex situations, but the principles are the same. As we become aware, we accept and acknowledge our feelings without judgment. We consider what the emotions might be telling us and try to use our best wisdom to choose how to respond actively to our emotions.

Mutual submission

Submission is not a very popular word in today's culture. Too often we have seen those with power directly or indirectly asking for submission from those they exploit. Yet we all know that, sometimes, submission can be a relief. We're tired of fighting and resisting all the time. Perhaps we recognize that we have wasted a lot of effort trying to change people who are not likely to change, at least in response to our forceful efforts.

I would suggest that the heart of submission is not about giving up what is rightfully ours, but, rather, accepting and supporting another's separate existence. It is more about the gracious acceptance of another's boundaries than a sacrifice of our own (though we may need to guard our boundaries less rigidly). If we are able to do that, we have gone a long way toward healthy submission.

The best submission, of course, is mutual submission. We see this when we remain in a stance of intentional vulnerability in our relationships. When others respond in kind to our risk-taking, we grow in trust, making ongoing mutual submission easier. When others don't treat our vulnerability well, we proceed with more caution.

Since we are so often insecure in our relationships, we tend to avoid this vulnerability, seeking with all kinds of nefarious creativity, actively or passively, to manipulate and control others—to gain power over them. This is the opposite of mutual submission.

A part of making submission an easier choice is to fully admit and let go of our tendency to demand our own way. During the countless times when our personal boundaries collide with another's, we can choose not to assume that our own boundaries are the ones that should be protected. Neither should we assume that we will always give in. Rather, in places of conflict, we can commit to a mutual process of seeking the best outcome. Demanding that others change according to our needs has a guaranteed failure rate.

We can be incredibly stubborn about not accepting others as they are. We think, somehow, that we have the ability, or even the right, to demand that people become what they are not. Even quiet, passive people often make these demands of others in the context of their inner thoughts and feelings. If the change we demand were simply a single behaviour, we might actually see the change take place one day. But so often we think others should change their very personality or orientation to life, forgetting how deeply set, perhaps even biological, these traits are. For example, one of the most fundamental aspects of maturity for many people is accepting that their parents are not likely to change their fundamental ways of being. They are who they are. Perhaps some of their annoying habits will one day soften, or a changing circumstance will permit a key insight. It may even be possible that a miraculous life change will take place, but in most cases it is an acceptance of others, rather than a pressure to change, that makes personal growth possible.

My wife, Carol, and I are both strong-willed people. Yet, somehow, we've managed to forge a marriage in which we fight so seldom that it's almost embarrassing to admit as a family counsellor. I haven't spent much personal time in the kind of territory I have to guide couples through in my counselling practice. I suspect that there is a complex blend of reasons why this was possible for us, but I think one key reason was stumbling into taking the risk of mutual submission from the beginning. Particularly through the early years of our marriage, we were gentle about making demands on each other. Most notably there was a time when my brother and I began getting excited about the idea of moving from central Canada to the Maritimes, and Carol (at the time my fiancée) did not get the excitement. Intuitively, I guessed that it would be a mistake to work at convincing her. By the time we headed eastward on our mad adventure a few years later, she was ready and didn't feel pressured.

While practising mutual submission, we can still value our own boundaries and sometimes allow others to experience the natural consequences of their behaviour. Submission does not mean a weak passivity or the careless enabling of another's harmful actions. We may need to confront with compassion and clarity, but we do so with respect, fully accepting others with their own personalities and histories. As much as possible, we avoid the imposition of power as we express ourselves.

Embracing the desert

As we try to give up the need to control others, we may easily find that this creates painful gaps. People will not meet our needs on our own schedule. Many of us, perhaps all of us at some level, will be tempted to find shortcuts to avoid feeling the pain of these gaps. When these shortcuts become habits that are hard to break, we might call them addictions.

In my counselling practice, I don't do a great deal of work with substance use or addictions, but the limited work I do in this area was transformed when I read a book by Gerald May called *Addiction and Grace*. In particular, when I shared one key insight highlighted by May, the freedom experienced by a client convinced me that this should become a central piece of my response to addictions in general—both the pervasive addictions associated with substance abuse and the "ordinary" addictions many of us struggle with (screens, sweets, sexual thoughts, etc.). May referred to the importance of loving our longing or learning to "tolerate spaciousness." I often refer to this as embracing the desert, encouraging people to interpret their feelings of emptiness and pain as part of the experience of healing.

By default, we often interpret the pain of emptiness or hungers of various kinds as deprivation, as evidence that we are unloved, rejected, or losers in the game of life. When, on the other hand, we are able to interpret this "spaciousness" positively, we are able to tap into a whole new pool of resources with which to tolerate the pain. We become hopeful that the endurance will lead to growth. We find courage to believe that we are accepting something that is genuinely, deeply, good. We trust that we are passing through this desert for the sake of others and ourselves, rather than wandering lost through an externally imposed exile or punishment.

Those of us who have been spared more serious and debilitating addictions don't usually realize the depth of the pain and craving that characterizes the desert for an alcoholic or meth addict. For them, the desert often looks endless, bleak, and lifeless. Who can imagine the amount of grace required to begin to trust that it's truly worth journeying through this wilderness when an escape to a quick relief or pleasure can promise to end the waiting. Living in a culture where consumerism and advertising have trained us all to expect instant gratification does not help.

In an earlier chapter, fasting was mentioned as a part of the rhythm of celebration. When we are a part of communities that value fasting, it helps us to build the expectation that seasons of emptiness and hunger are a natural part of the rhythm of life. This could be a day without food or a season (like Lent) without the more immediately gratifying types of food. A community that supports the avoidance of casual sex and encourages the reserving of a fully sexual relationship for when there is commitment and stability practises another sort of fasting. Friends who encourage each other to live simpler lifestyles in order to support development in poverty-stricken areas or in order to ease the burden on the planet are also fasting. As it becomes normal in our life together to experience these fasts, we will know a lot more about how to support each other in embracing the desert because we will all know the experience and the value of emptiness and of waiting, alone and together.

Believing in enough

One fundamental belief can strongly undergird our ability to embrace the desert: the belief that there is enough to go around. We are not living in a world of scarcity in which we have to compete, or oppress others, in order to survive. This belief can extend from basic resources like food and shelter all the way to love. This is a belief that must be a shared belief. No one can say to a parent of starving children, "just believe that there is enough." Yet we know that even with a global population exceeding seven billion, the earth can produce enough for everyone, if we could only distribute the abundance with compassion. Violent conflict and unfair economic competition, not lack of food, creates the starvation in our world.

Gandhi famously wrote, "There is enough for everyone's need, but there is not enough for everyone's greed." More recently, voices like Millard Fuller (founder of Habitat for Humanity) and Shane Claiborne have emphasized how a "theology of enough" can turn our shared lives around. This belief can be one of the most practical ways in which we learn to live from a place of trust rather than fear. If we really believe that there is enough to go around, we can create communities that choose trust and open-handed sharing, rather than individualistic striving and competition for limited resources.

Some see this principle behind the gospel stories of the feeding of the crowds. I'm not intending to belittle the possibility of supernatural help, but I find it inspiring to wonder if what happened when Jesus encouraged the first meagre resources to be shared, was that everyone began sharing what they had. When it seems as though there is not enough to go around, miracles can happen if people choose to trust and share rather than hoard out of fear.

A negative example, a warning tale, can be found in Leo Tolstoy's short story, "How Much Land Does a Man Need?" In this story, we read of a peasant, Pahom, whose inability to be content with enough comes to undo all of his ambition. Always striving for more, he is elated at the prospect of a great deal he is offered: for a few roubles he can own all the land he can walk around in a day as long as he completes the circuit by sunset. In the end, though his greed makes him choose far too much land, he just manages to complete the circuit only to fall down dead from exhaustion. We see that a man *needs* only the six feet of earth required to bury him.

It may seem like a radical leap to start trusting that there is enough. Perhaps the first step is gratefully receiving what one has—choosing contentment, imagining that it just might be enough. Then we can take further steps of beginning to share what we have, trusting that we will still have enough. When we see the fruit of these choices, a deep belief that there really is enough, that the world is a place of abundance and not scarcity, may take root. This belief is a powerful act of acceptance in response to life. As we believe in it more and more deeply, we can feel ourselves relax and open up to life and others.

Acceptance may seem to be a restrained rhythm, but there is a deep joy and peace in being content with what one has, with who one is, and with the reality that surrounds us. We are open-eyed, aware that pain, frustration, and disappointment are also a part of this contentment. Yet our contentment holds firm. And, as we slip over the thin line between being content and actually delighting in ourselves, delighting in our neighbours and delighting in our world, we are brought back, full circle, to celebration.

Getting Practical

Practise emotional mindfulness. On a day in which you have some troubling emotions, take a quiet moment to review the feelings that happened in you, without judgment. Acknowledge and accept the feelings as gifts that will help you to understand yourself better. Take time to be curious about what beliefs and perspectives helped create those emotions. Imaginatively hold the emotions tenderly for a time (even, perhaps, visualize holding the emotions in your cradled hands) and then let them go.

Practise compassionate presence. Consider the person you know that is the most powerful embodiment of compassion. Some people might imagine the real, yet abstract, presence of God, but most of us need to imagine such Presence in a personified form—perhaps imagining Jesus, or more contemporary examples of people unusually filled with a divine compassion. Practise contemplating, visualizing, this person's love and perspective being actually present with you, being shared with you. As you practise this more and more, see how it can transform recollections of hard moments in your day, moments when you responded badly to others or they responded badly to you. Listen, be open, to new insights that emerge; let your imagination shift your hardened perspectives. Perhaps eventually, this will even heal some memories of hurt or shame, though for really painful memories, you would probably be wise to have a caring, experienced person share in this exercise with you.

Dialogue with your selves. If you notice yourself in the midst of an inner struggle, see if you can identify two or three different parts of yourself that are trying to be heard. Give them names and journal a dialogue between these "selves." You might be sure to include a voice that represents your best, wisest self and/or an internalized voice of a wise elder, or even your best intuition of the inner, still voice of God. Make sure also to hear, respect and care for the more shadowy voices (such as angry or selfish voices). It's not necessarily important to carry the dialogue through to resolution but continue it enough to become more aware of the inner dialogue that is taking place, getting a better understanding of how that relates to the given struggle.

Engage in relaxation exercises. Many people learning to deal with their anger or anxiety have been taught relaxation exercises. These range from breathing exercises to visualization to progressive muscle relaxation. All are excellent practices focused largely on our bodies, and different exercises will work best for each person. The calming and soothing results of these exercises can help us with acceptance, and can be combined with practising more direct mental efforts to accept ourselves and others.

THE ACTIVE RHYTHMS

The Active Rhythms

The first three rhythms discussed were the rhythms of response: they represent the basic ways in which we respond to life with its joys and sorrows, its realities and possibilities. This next set of rhythms describes how we actively participate in and transform our worlds. They have to do with the major ways in which we find and create meaning in our lives.

The three rhythms into which I'll categorize our active responses are good work, embracing others and journeying together. The first of these emphasizes our need for embodied and purposeful engagement with the world. The second discusses our primary social attitudes and practices, and the third, growing out of the other two, focuses on the intentionality of a journey together. On this journey we invite others to join us as we walk toward wholeness, toward a more just and peaceful world. The active rhythms are all seasoned by the responsive rhythms and lead to the final and most inclusive rhythm of yearning for home.

4 GOOD WORK

Good human work honors God's work. Good work uses no thing without respect, both for what it is in itself and for its origin. It uses neither tool nor material that it does not respect and that it does not love. It honors nature as a great mystery and power, as an indispensable teacher, and as the inescapable judge of all work of human hands. It does not dissociate life and work, or pleasure and work, or love and work, or usefulness and beauty. To work without pleasure or affection, to make a product that is not both useful and beautiful, is to dishonor God, nature, the thing that is made, and whomever it is made for.

– Wendell Berry

Imagine a woman in her mid-50s who is forced to retire early after a small stroke. For more than 20 years she had worked as a middle manager for a large company that made a wide variety of products that, for the most part, she considered pointless. But it paid well.

Now, after a challenging rehabilitation that had involved walking many hours through city streets and parks, she realized that she was starting to enjoy her days more than she had while working in her stressful office. And this in spite of the deep frustrations she currently had with her sluggish right arm and leg. When she started supplementing her disability pension by putting out ads to walk dogs, she added a new purpose to her walks. From the dogs and their owners, she experienced more appreciation now than she had as a manager in spite of a successful reputation. Most days she came home tired but happy.

~

One of our greatest needs as human beings is to be engaged in embodied, purposeful activity, and this is what I am referring to as good work. We need to be engaged in producing tangible results on a day-to-day level that make some kind of meaningful contribution for ourselves, our families and others. In spite of all the so-called improvements in our quality of life, many of us have great difficulty finding opportunities for such good work.

Our contemporary society places many barriers between us and good work. We think or hope there is some meaning involved in our work, but we are often uncertain of its value or of our role in the final outcome. Our bodies are increasingly separated from our work by screens, by anonymous mass culture, by robotic machinery and by systems of bureaucracy or corporate hierarchies. Those with the energy and the space are usually more satisfied with their weekend work in the garden than their 40 hours at the office.

Understanding our need for good work can help us explore the connection between our natural ecosystems and our local communities. This integration can help us to find a better balance between creative ambition and a wise understanding of limits, including the vital human need to rest. Resting well is much more satisfying after good work. Our culture is hungry for better work and better rest.

Disconnection, boredom and unemployment

There are many signs of the disconnection from good work in our present world. Two of the more obvious and visible symptoms are boredom and unemployment. It is tragic that there is so much boredom and unemployment when there is so much good work to be done.

Unemployment, of course, is the more serious of the two. The literal poverty it creates is only the tip of the iceberg. It takes a huge toll on our identity, our family life and our search for meaning. The vague but real damage to our psyche is revealed by the fact that even when financially cared for, we will tend to volunteer less rather than more after we lose our jobs. Our energy and ability to engage with life and with others is sapped by the loss of a sense of our place in this world, not to mention the natural fears and insecurities for the future.

One of the deepest justice issues for any society is the obligation to provide the opportunity for good work, and one of the delusions of capitalism is the belief that this obligation is met by a competitive open market. The success stories of the few who are able to respond to harsh poverty by working hard and becoming wealthy is misinterpreted to mean that such opportunities exist for all who are willing to make the effort. This is a huge denial of the nature of personality and other practical limitations. Only a fraction of people have the psychological or physical raw material to pull themselves up by their bootstraps with their creativity and entrepreneurial spirit. The free market argument is like a man with a smug smile standing on top of a deep pit full of people. Seeing those tall enough and strong enough climb out of the pit, he says, "See, anyone can climb out if they really want to," ignoring the small or frail who are being stepped on by the others.

On the other hand, once adequate work is possible so that our most basic needs are met, there are few barriers to a reasonable chance of happiness. A society that is able to provide consistent opportunities for basic, good work is likely to be a content and relatively harmonious society, as long as the gap between rich and poor, powerful and weak, is kept from stretching too far. Some elasticity is necessary—perfect equality is not a reasonable or even worthwhile goal. There will always be some with more ambition, more energy and more desires in life, while others would prefer to be content with less stuff, less activity and less stress.

The ancient Jewish concept of Jubilee is a rare example of an economic model (perhaps only a theory – hard to know how well it was ever implemented) based on that kind of flexibility. This model allowed those who worked hard and managed well to thrive and expand their territory, but it prevented the inequalities from hardening over generations. Every 50 years, debts were forgiven, slaves were freed, and land was returned to the original family lines. It was not a perfect system, nor one suited (without creative adaptation) for our times, but we desperately need economic models that stop the gap between rich and poor from spiralling out of control, and we need to make a priority of ensuring that everyone has the opportunity for good work.

While boredom might especially be a problem for the unemployed, it is oddly common even among the overworked. Since work is often disembodied and experientially meaningless, we are bored at work, and when we're not at work, we are listless and passive unless entertained or diverted. Having become so alienated from community, from the natural world, and from work that is integrated with all of life, we need to make up for this disconnection with novelty, stimulation and entertainment. But what we are craving most is satisfied when we find work in any context that is deeply engaging and connected with effective results.

Recent research indicates the counterintuitive finding that boredom is a state of stress, resulting from people interpreting their lack of stimulation as "something wrong." In other words, boredom has to do with not giving oneself permission to rest—our inactivity or lack of stimulation is perceived inwardly as a problem. In fact, there seems to be a strong correlation between boredom and addiction, though we don't know in which direction the causation flows. Boredom might lead people to seek addictive substances or the nature of addiction might lead to a significant increase in the experience of boredom whenever not stimulated by artificial means.

Another less surprising aspect of boredom is that it is associated with lack of movement: we are more bored when our bodies are not moving. So another reason we are more bored today is that our lives are far too sedentary. We sit for far too long. Medical problems including increased risk of heart attacks are associated with sitting too long without regular movement. For those who can, good work means getting off of our butts as much as we can.

Embodied work

Unfortunately, given the link between mental and physical health and body movement, a sad reality of our technological age is that an increasing percentage of our work has become dis-embodied. Many of us work with our eyes on a screen and our fingers on a keyboard, but the rest of our bodies contribute little.

We then choose to continue this in the way we order our domestic lives. We often run from the few potential bits of physical labour that remain. We hire someone for the hard work, purchase labour-saving devices and drive anywhere we can. Of course, this necessitates paying for gym memberships or purchasing exercise equipment in order to do what we can with the flabby bodies that result. When the lazier part of me is tempted to avoid walking or doing some physical labour, I often remind myself that these tasks are one way I care for my body (though, after I hit about 45, I found this argument with myself no longer inspired me when friends ask me to move heavy furniture).

As life and work "progress" to take place more and more in a virtual environment, it will become increasingly necessary to be intentional about keeping as much of our activity and socializing as embodied as possible. This will mean making occasional choices for inefficiency and for less alluring options, which I suspect will often turn out to be more deeply efficient and alluring than they might have seemed on the surface.

When it comes to the kind of human service work that many of us are engaged in, embodiment means prioritizing face-to-face interaction over against electronic communication. We are now able to have quick and free video interactions over the Internet, but we should not equate this with being in the same room. The word "screen" itself implies a barrier: something comes between

> ### Why Walking Will Save You
>
> 1. It brings you into solidarity with people across time, across the world, across all people groups.
> 2. It slows you down.
> 3. It gives you space to notice what's around you, and think or pray.
> 4. It doesn't exploit the world's resources.
> 5. It doesn't pollute or increase global warming.
> 6. It connects you with the natural world and the seasons.
> 7. It connects you with the community in which you live.
> 8. It gives you healthy, gentle exercise.
> 9. It provides the opportunity to bump into people.
> 10. It provides you with vitamin D.
> 11. It's a great way to converse with a fellow walker.
> 12. It increases dependence on the local economy.
> 13. It's a spiritual discipline—like fasting.

us and the other person. And this barrier comes at a cost. It separates us, distances us, from the people we engage with virtually. Interaction via screen is a very watered-down version of human contact.

In the early days of the Internet, there was great excitement about how all the new opportunities for human contact would improve the lives of those who, for a variety of reasons, were not very socially engaged. Now, many studies have looked at the effects of virtual communication on the quality of relationships and mood. The results are not encouraging: generally they show an increase in depression and alienation as more time is spent online, even when primarily using so-called social media. While some people really do emotionally benefit from virtual connections such as social media, the biggest gains are for those who use virtual communication to increase the amount and quality of their direct human interaction.

The fact is that we experience people quite differently when we are physically present with them. All of our senses are engaged. Even when not physically touching, our bodies are involved.

Focal things and practices

One approach to the concept of good work in our current age that emphasizes embodiment, among other things, is the work of a philosopher of technology, Albert Borgmann. A central concept arising from his work is that of "focal things" as opposed to "devices." In an interview with David Wood, Borgmann states:

> A focal thing is something that has a commanding presence, engages your body and mind, and engages you with others. Focal things and the kinds of engagements they foster have the power to center your life, and to arrange all other things around this center in an orderly way because you know what's important and what's not. A focal practice results from committed engagement with the focal thing.

Devices, on the other hand, are severed from any historical or local context. As a result, we have no idea how we have come to be dependent on any particular device, and we typically don't think or care about the people in the Asian factory who manufactured it. The devices are a means to an end without much inherent meaning or value. They can even be "hyper-real." Such devices overcome natural limitations or inconveniences in a way that ends up disconnecting us even further from the natural world, creating expectations of unsustainably unreal environments. Devices aren't necessarily evil or bad; they're just not as rich, meaningful, or holistically engaging as focal things. If we choose them too often, we thin out or flatten our lives.

Focal things create engagement with focal practices. These practices require commitment: we need to learn the skills and knowledge that enable their successful, ongoing use. They usually involve more engagement with our bodies. Often, focal practices require more interdependence within our communities.

Borgmann's classic example is that of how we heat our houses. A woodstove is a focal thing. In order to use it to heat our house, we need to understand its safe installation in our home. We need to find a source of firewood—often via a human relationship with someone who manages a local and sustainable woodlot. People often joke about wood "heating twice" (or three times) because of the work required to chop, stack and carry it. It makes a mess and takes daily effort to get a fire started.

However, it creates warmth from a central and, usually, attractive place. It draws households together around a more life-giving centre than a television. It doesn't waste heat on unused rooms. Since it's cool in the mornings and in the extremities of the house, we remember that it's winter and dress appropriately—connecting us to the season.

Thermostats and furnaces, on the other hand, are devices. When we're cold, we twist a dial and that's that. We care little about the furnace as long as it runs, and we probably don't have a clue who delivers the oil (or who checks our gas meter). There is no engagement, no centre, and a disconnection from the realities of winter (depending, of course, on how much we care about the monthly heating bill). Many of us even walk around our homes in mid-winter in short sleeves and bare feet. And none of this is necessarily wrong; but the more these devices replace focal things, the more our lives thin out, and we become disengaged from central facets of life (like the nature of heat in winter).

Good work should also have the tendency to pull us away from consumerism—perhaps because we make less money, perhaps because we choose to get engaged in focal practices that reduce our need for devices. The more my wife and I have been intentional about growing and preparing quality food (thankfully out of love for cooking more than any moral effort), the more we have come to ignore large portions of the supermarket. Buying processed and prepared foods seems like such a poor (and over-salted) imitation of what we would much rather create together at home from ingredients that we grew or purchased from local sources.

Integration with communities and environment

The book of Genesis is rich with deep understandings of the nature of work. We find here that work is a divine task. God's work began with the stuff of creation, and the first task assigned to humanity was to take care of this created world. We are seen, in fact, as partners in God's ongoing creative work, implying that human vocations are patterned after the Creator's work.

So good work is creative, though not, or at least not necessarily, in the sense of the novelty of an idea—something new out of nothing—but in the sense of work being an ongoing part of finding and working with the balance of order and chaos in the world around us.

In simpler societies, past and present, the connection between working well with the natural environment and the sustaining of families and communities is obvious. Most roles in such societies involve working in cooperation with the natural order. Fundamentally, and perhaps metaphorically, good work makes us think of such tasks as gathering, hunting, cultivation, animal husbandry, waste management, etc. It may sound like basing the idea of good work on these practices idealizes the "primitive" or suggests a naïve romanticization of the "back-to-the-land" movement. But to the extent that we cannot trace our work (and technology) back to their connections with these foundations, I believe our work clearly becomes "not good." We are as dependent as ever on working within earthly ecosystems, and those who forget this are the ones who are most deeply, and dangerously, naïve.

We continue to expand an understanding of good work by looking at how our communities are best served upon that foundation. We require artisans to craft and develop ways to enhance our lives as individuals, families and communities—to build functional, comfortable and beautiful shelter or to provide the equipment and furnishings needed to make our work and leisure enjoyable. We need artists to inspire and to provide new lenses with which to see and interact with what is around us. We need musicians and storytellers to invite us to remember where to find meaning and how to tap into the deep rhythms that draw us together. We need to clean and organize our homes and common spaces. We need wise observers of human, spiritual and natural patterns to help us guide our actions. There are countless other ways in which good work is manifested in our service to one another: care for the sick and for children, providing transportation, preparing food, teaching skills and knowledge, etc.

We can understand the integration of these tasks with our natural and human communities when we consider that the words "economy" and "ecology" are both linked to the Greek work for household (*oikos*). They both refer to the study of systems in which the health of our households is sustained, implying an interaction and interdependence on social bonds and trade, and on sustainably creating a niche in our natural environments. How ironic that these words rooted in the common household now tend to be used for systems that are so huge and complicated that we've become overwhelmed and detached. Few of us understand how it can make sense that we've created entities "too big to fail," allowing their broken exploitation of individuals to continue. In spite of the massive scale and the complexity now implied, the words "economy" and "ecology" are still ultimately about how our households integrate with those around us.

Even in our technological age, many of us are still fortunate enough that we can see how our vocations fit within this root meaning of economy/ecology, providing motivation and encouragement to invest energy and persevere in these tasks. For many others, however, there are layers and layers of abstraction and justification required to get from our daily tasks to any connection with root values. As a young man, I worked for a couple of years at a large taxation data centre. As soon as I stepped through the door, flashing my nametag in order to prove my right to be there, I entered a depersonalized world. Sitting in a quad of desks, among a sea of such quads and cubicles, we would get to work. I recall sitting there, no windows or natural light anywhere nearby, and thought about how relatively little sense it made to believe in God (or even nature!) in the midst of this artificial environment. That thought never occurs to me in a garden.

When we find ourselves in occupations that are abstracted from the wild and natural world (even when we are successful at tracing a meaning back to a good and useful purpose), then we need to ground ourselves in other intentional ways. To garden, to prepare a fabulous meal for others, to produce something beautiful or useful with our hands—these are not just hobbies. They remind us of the purpose of work. Work is meant to bring about a good and visible result even when not rewarded with a paycheque. A paycheque should not provide the meaning of work but enable us to continue doing this good work for its own sake.

Good work in a corporate age

While much of what I am describing probably implies (correctly) that I doubt that much good work can easily be found in the midst of our corporate culture, I do want to address part of this question directly. In our technological age, corporations are quite probably, to some degree, a necessary evil. However, I do feel justified (and not just spiteful or political) in calling them inherently evil because of the way that they are intentionally designed to be contrary to the model of good work I am describing. They are bound by law to be centred around the purpose of creating profit for their shareholders. That does not lead naturally to good work. As the book and documentary, *The Corporation*, demonstrated so well, corporations are legal "persons" who by definition (though certainly with some exceptions) fit the psychological profile of psychopaths: self-serving and uncaring about the feelings of others while they evade responsibility and natural consequences as much as possible.

I see two essential problems with the corporate world (and I'm sure there are many more). One is that it separates the owners (shareholders) from all the nasty details of their work. So we have a world full of shareholders who are often caring, thoughtful people in their local communities, blissfully unaware that they are engaged in exploiting the weak and the environment around the globe in order to produce profits that fund their "innocent" and "well-deserved" retirement. The second is that it is very, very difficult to deal in a consistently thoughtful and humane way on a massive scale. The sheer size of corporations and the work they do usually creates inhumane work environments that don't have the flexibility and sensitivity to deal with unique problems and to respond quickly to mistakes.

Personally, I try to keep as many dollars as I possibly can out of corporate hands and systems, but I know this avoidance can only go so far. So I also believe we need new corporate laws and regulations that will see corporations constitutionally required to balance their profit motive with the need to be ecologically sustainable and with the mandate to care well for their employees and consumers as well as shareholders. There are actually people working at such responsible economic models and they need our support.

Limits and rest

The more our work is engaged locally with our communities and with the environment, the more we should naturally be aware of the limits of our work. The concept of limits has had a bad rap in a world focused on ambition and ever-increasing growth. But just as was mentioned in the earlier chapter on acceptance, the awareness and acceptance of the limits of our work is a source of hope and peace.

It is not good for us to be competitively striving for more and more. We don't need higher "qualities of life" the way they are often measured. The true sources of a quality life are found in sustainable communities, not in an increasing amount of stuff.

Except in nations oppressed by foreign powers and by local violence and corruption, we don't require more technology, even better health care, for a quality life. People aren't happier and more fulfilled because life expectancy is increased by a couple of years spent in sheltered nursing homes. We have no idea what the true costs are (for the poor, for the global economy, etc.) of developing immensely costly life-prolonging procedures that we will never be able to afford to provide for everyone. I believe that technological ambition does at least as much damage as it does good in our contemporary world, largely because it is often seen as freeing us from limits more than helping us do our best within them or even appropriately expanding them.

One of the most ancient concepts that offers the reminder of the gift of limits is the Jewish concept of the Sabbath: the seventh day, devoted to rest. We need rest. But for rest to be fully satisfying and restorative, we need to embrace it. This won't happen if we're frustrated at the work we're not doing and the dollars we're not earning as we rest.

Trust is a key to good rest. We must trust and accept that the work that we are doing on the other days is enough. We need to trust that there are other crucial aspects to life besides work. So rest allows us to slow down and pay attention to what might otherwise be forgotten on the days when we are either working or too weary and frazzled to think. Momentum is gaining in many circles for the practise of technology Sabbaths, shutting down our screens and devices as much as possible one day a week. We can attend instead to life and love and meaning—matters of spirit and faith. We can be fully present to the people we live with and near. We can be more deliberate in our celebrating, lamenting and accepting practices. Rest is a time to regain perspective—something easily lost if our work is too frantic, competitive and meaningless.

The hero and the settler

One polarity related to good work that I have not yet mentioned is the archetypal tension between the work of the hero and the work of the settler. It is most likely the work of the settler that first comes to mind in a chapter on work, as we tend to envision the settled life with its daily and seasonal necessities when we think of work. The work of heroes, on the other hand, is filled (at least when seen from afar or in retrospect) with adventure and spontaneous action.

While there are certainly personalities more inclined toward one or the other, I will suggest that we all have some need to be engaged in both. Once more, the tension needs to be resolved in the form of some kind of rhythm, though I will also discuss ways in which the two are sometimes more integrated than might be obvious.

Heroism has to do with themes like leaving home and overcoming new obstacles, finding new possibilities and saving those in distress. There is usually a push and/or a pull involved in such heroism, as the hero may be drawn out by the depth of the need or the abundance of the opportunity, or the hero may feel compelled to leave home by the drive for change and adventure.

In our day, this is less likely to look like St. George slaying a dragon and more likely to look like a young woman striking out with Doctors without Borders or some other overseas NGO in order to "make a difference." Or this might be the middle-aged bureaucrat who leaves the safe suburbs to chat with homeless men at a shelter. Or a young family leaves the city and buys a homestead with two other families to start an intentional community. Spiritually, their task is more prophetic than priestly, speaking with clarity about new interpretations and necessary awareness about a coming fork in the road.

The work of the settler is equally important. Settlers provide stability in their families and communities. Their tasks require at least as much trustworthiness and faithfulness as the hero, but their focus is steadfast commitment over the long haul, rather than the shining moment. Their creativity is demonstrated less in bursts of insight and more in the results that are built up over time.

Settlers, then, create communities and nurture healthy networks of relationships. They demonstrate the beauty and necessity of commitment to relationships, to the land, to rootedness. They nurse wounded heroes back to life and rebuild the structural damage caused by literal and metaphorical revolutions. Spiritually, they are the faithful priests who maintain life-giving traditions and liturgical forms.

The point is that good work sometimes requires leaving the familiar and the settled and facing the challenges of change and the unknown, while other good work requires steady commitment, persisting in the face of sameness and weariness. It is a gift to our world that some personalities are drawn to one and others to the opposite. I have known men and women who have worked at the same repetitive job (that I would find mind-numbing) for decades and have been quite content. I have known others who quite intentionally are always on the move or take on tasks of incredible risk, which, when I think of them, make me glad to be puttering in my garden at home.

However, this welcome truth of the diversity of gifts should not leave us too imbalanced in our own lives. While each of us may be best suited to one or the other, good work at times will require us all to know both. Settlers will all be called out to heroic moments wherein they courageously embrace change, perhaps even risking all they have built up over time. Heroes will be called to seasons of rootedness and commitment, at least temporarily sacrificing their restless need to seek adventure and fight the enemy.

Of course from the *Odyssey* onward, we clearly see these two aspects of good work reflected in literature. Tolkien's *Lord of the Rings* trilogy is a classic example. From the solidly rooted peace of the Shire's hobbits to the healing refuge of elfin Rivendell, there are beautiful depictions of the importance and need for settled work. The "fellowship of the ring" are those ready to take up the heroic challenge of journey and battle, including those who long for this (like Gimli) and those who would much rather be smoking a pipe in the Shire (like Samwise Gamgee). While riveting stories tend to be biased toward adventure, and *The Lord of the Rings* is no exception, we clearly see the rhythmic need for both heroes and settlers. We also see the value in each type experiencing seasons of the opposite task.

In many historical examples, we can also see that the two kinds of work are often more integrated than we might otherwise expect. Now that we are many decades past the '60s, we tend to look back and see the heroism involved in the civil rights movement—the risks and striking rhetoric of Martin Luther King, or the brilliant spontaneity of Rosa Parks. It wasn't until I saw the documentary series, *A Force More Powerful*, that I learned of the long-term, intentional planning and preparation that was a part of the effectiveness of this movement. In church basements and community halls, pastors and leaders dedicated to nonviolence taught and trained young men and women, black and white, in the ways of nonviolent resistance. They carefully studied and planned to see where and how their efforts and symbolic acts would make the most difference. They rehearsed responses to the taunts and violence they knew would be a part of ignoring the segregation of downtown lunch counters. They prepared for the emotional and economic support that would enable them to handle the prison terms they knew would come. Heroes and settlers who work together change the world.

Good work is the engine of a good life. It knits together the body, mind and spirit; it knits together our families, communities and ecosystems. When this engine operates smoothly and consistently, it will be a great deal easier for the other elements of a good life to fall into place.

Getting Practical

Grow something. There is great value in growing something. Even if it's just a token herb on a kitchen windowsill, it reminds us of what is involved in the production of food and the sustaining of life. The act of cultivation reminds us that our sustenance is based on natural systems that are fragile and yet miraculous. If we have room for a small kitchen garden, we can remind ourselves what food is meant to taste like and come to appreciate the farmers' market more than the supermarket.

Make or fix something. In our complicated world, we often feel that everything is made in factories and only experts fix things. Consider what useful thing you might do with your hands. Can you look online for instructions and fix that old appliance instead of buying a new one? Can you think of anything that would enhance your life or your household that you could produce yourself?

Re-evaluate lifestyle. With your spouse or in a family meeting or with some close friends, raise the question of whether intentionally choosing to embrace a simpler lifestyle would enable more life-giving work. What would it take to make that simpler lifestyle work? Would others join you or support you in this adventure?

5 EMBRACING THE OTHER

*...open arms are a sign that I have created space in
myself for the other to come in
and that I have made a movement out of myself
so as to enter the space created by the other...*

– Miroslav Volf

Imagine a successful corporate executive with a daughter that frustrated him immensely during her rebellious teen years. Things only got worse when she went to university, becoming an environmental engineer with radically anti-corporate political views. When she expressed her views, he heard only disgust directed toward him. After years of barely speaking, at a dinner awkwardly forced by his wife, he looks across the table and realizes that his love for his daughter has been almost completely overshadowed by his disappointment, hurt and frustration. He knows he has been a large part of the problem, and he resolves to see her with new eyes, to open the door to a new possibility of relationship. For the first time in ages, he lets himself make eye contact with her and gives a sad smile.

The next day, meeting in a café, he invites her to share the passions that guide her. He actually listens and realizes that much of what she believes makes sense. He also sees that the tone of disgust he used to hear in her voice "all the time" only came when he was being defensive of his company. She had hated perceiving him as a pawn of the corporate powers. By the end of their encounter, they had even begun tentatively exploring things that he might do differently if he considered her point of view. When she left, she gave him a quick embrace and he felt a lightness in his heart that he hadn't felt for 10 years.

~

One of the greatest obstacles of the good life is the difficulty we have in accepting people who have the annoying tendency to be different from us or to remind us of the things that we don't want to accept in ourselves. Yet overcoming this difficulty is so rewarding. We hear teachers joke, "I'd love my job if I didn't have to work with students," while simultaneously knowing that the fulfilment of their work is not so much in the concepts but in the real relationships that form in the classroom. Quite probably, their most fulfilling moment happened with the kid who was initially a pain in the neck.

Fear and laziness lead us to want to shut out people whose ideas, behaviours or very existence challenge something in our own lives. We don't like the change, the effort or the risk that are required whenever we really let ourselves encounter the stranger or the enemy. Even with the people closest to us, we are often threatened by their "otherness." To protect ourselves, we withdraw or manipulate or dominate in order to control the space around us and keep ourselves safe. But, of course, this is not safety at all but the beginning of deep loneliness and alienation.

When we can embrace the other, the one we perceive as different from us, we find that in spite of the real challenges, risks and work required, embrace adds an important spice and variety to our life.

Until relatively recently, I used to see squash as my enemy. A bad introduction in my childhood, involving very real gagging at the dinner table, made me consider it a worthless vegetable. After years of resistance, I sampled my wife's squash soup and my mind was opened. Then I sautéed some yellow summer squash in butter and garlic and was impressed by the wonderful, nutty taste. Through my adolescent years I'd also been deeply suspicious of mushrooms, onions and green peppers. Now all of these are among my most favourite foods. I've embraced my enemies and my life is richer for it.

Another way to refer to our need to embrace others is to insist that we dedicate ourselves to the humanization of all others. Built into the language of many ethnic groups is the notion that "people" are those who are within one's group. Those beyond the borders are not people—not yet accepted as fully human. But the world is now too small for this kind of ethnocentrism.

There are many ways in which we dehumanize others: withholding empathy; deliberately misinterpreting the motivations of others; judging others as more primitive or less developed and their religious practices as demonic; de-personalizing a culture (forgetting that real individuals, including women and children, are part of the group); maintaining and spreading negative and degrading stereotypes. During times of war, the "need" for propaganda reveals the natural resistance we feel to the horrors of mass violence and chaos. New soldiers have such a natural tendency to abhor killing other humans that they must be trained to dehumanize the enemy. Or they are kept in planes (or operating drones), high above enemies who have become merely "targets."

Closer to home, there are many commercial and political temptations for harnessing fear through dehumanization. Liberals are baby-killers who live lives of wanton immorality. Conservatives are backwater rednecks who are armed to the teeth and obviously never think. The streets are filled with criminals that you need to protect yourself against. The marketplace is full of competitive cutthroats so you need to fight dirty or be a loser. All of these messages try to keep us from embracing the humanity of people with whom we are connected, whether they live near or far.

Embracing the enemy

Perhaps the most striking spiritual transition in the Judeo-Christian tradition occurred when Jesus taught his followers these words:

> 'You have heard that it was said, "You shall love your neighbour and hate your enemy." But I say to you, Love your enemies and pray for those who persecute you, so that you may be children of your Father in heaven; for he makes his sun rise on the evil and on the good, and sends rain on the righteous and on the unrighteous.... Be perfect, therefore, as your heavenly Father is perfect. (Matthew 5.43–45, 48)

Not only was Jesus challenging his followers to the unheard of goal of loving their enemies and persecutors, but he also stated that this was the means by which we reach true maturity ("perfection")—loving our enemies is how we become like God.

In typical fashion, Jesus told a story, the parable of the Good Samaritan, to drive this ethical invitation into resistant hearts. The story follows a question from a religious leader: "Who is our neighbour?" As we, who often have the same question in our minds, imaginatively listen, we are led into empathizing with the beaten and robbed man who is ignored by the good religious folks (a priest and a Levite) who are too preoccupied with their own concerns to care. We feel astonishing relief as the kind Samaritan turns out to be the one that takes the time and makes the effort to care, mercifully oblivious to the cultural enmity that might make him hesitate. The story forces us to ask ourselves the question, "When I am in real need, who would I like to consider me a neighbour? Would I like a Samaritan—an enemy (or at least an outsider)—to be neighbourly to me?" This is the story that clearly fleshes out the Golden Rule: the invitation to treat others as we would like to be treated.

In Jesus' world, as in many places today, one's enemies were a tangible part of one's daily life. In much of the Western world, we now live in such segregated and isolated ways that our serious enemies are almost like abstractions to us. Very few of us are ever face-to-face with those we would actually admit to calling enemies. So having suggested that embracing the other must go all the way to the extent of loving our enemy, let's turn back to those we actually live with.

Fear, control and trust

Most of us are threatened by difference. Our fears and insecurities rise to the surface when those with whom we are most vulnerable demonstrate the ways in which they are different from us. The differences of even a beloved "other" make our lives less predictable and controllable. Our comfortable perspectives may be challenged, our familiar patterns questioned. The weaknesses or judgments of others might expose our own weaknesses and judgments that we are ashamed of and don't want to admit.

One of the things that I love about the faith community that I'm a part of is its diversity. We think about other human beings and even God quite differently from one another, and yet we (usually) get along. One of the hardest parts for me, though, is when I come face-to-face with a point of view that I used to hold myself, but of which I am now ashamed. Seeing the narrow stance embarrasses me, and I have to admit to myself that these were my thoughts just a few years earlier. The hurt that I am afraid the other person might be causing with his judgments are the hurts I then admit that I have also caused. Then I have to wonder how many more of these blind spots are still at work in me.

On a simpler level, there is the bare fact that in any relationship or organization, those who think differently will want to do and plan things differently from what I would want. Whether in a marriage, a workplace, a community or a nation, these differences have to be negotiated. I will have to sacrifice some of the things I want to see happen. I will likely end up doing things or being a part of things that aren't my preference, from the relatively trivial (which TV show we watch) to those with serious repercussions (which laws my country creates and enforces).

One of the most typical responses to this difference we see all around us is to organize relationships around the dynamics of power and competition. One dominates and the other submits. Those who dominate often rationalize or deny this use of power. Those who submit sometimes deny their freedom and responsibility, their ability to relate any differently. Or the seemingly weaker party finds ways to manipulate "from below." The spiral of this unhealthy power dynamic is pervasive in our world at all levels.

Trust, on the other hand, transforms our response to difference. When we trust, then difference becomes the spice of life. Encountering the other enables us to change and to grow. Considering the different ways that others view life keeps our perspectives from becoming stale and entrenched, and helps us to see our blind spots. Sacrifice and compromise will definitely be a part of the picture, but what is gained will, in most cases, be worth the risk.

Risk is at the heart of growing in trust. Trust grows through a spiral that involves such dynamics as risk taking, communication, discernment/reflection, forgiveness and learning new perspectives. When any of these dynamics are missing, it will be hard for trust to grow, and we will be tempted to slip back toward power and competition.

Assertiveness

One of the words that often stands in for that complex spiral of skills and actions is assertiveness. This is especially true when that spiral of growing in trust is based on a healthy embrace of ourselves. While love may sometimes require that we endure loss or even violence rather than violate another, love does not include encouraging or inviting our own victimization. Assertiveness describes that balance of appropriately respecting and expressing our own needs and boundaries in such a way that they are most likely to be respected and accepted by others. In other words, assertiveness is the active side of the mutual submission described earlier. Empathy and compassion temper our assertiveness to help prevent it from becoming an excuse for selfishness. At times, an assertive response may even give voice to anger for the sake of transparency, but the result will be more honest and vulnerable than aggressive.

Without some assertiveness, the avoidance of conflict and anger will almost always lead to passive-aggression. Healthy assertiveness is so rare that in my counselling office I simply assume that someone who never expresses anger is passive-aggressive. Of course, many of those who occasionally explode with anger may also be passive-aggressive until they reach their boiling point.

Passive-aggression refers to the intentional or unintentional (even unconscious) ways in which we act out our annoyance or resentment without clearly expressing it or taking responsibility for it. Probably the most common way in which we do this is by withdrawing from a relationship, but it can also include such things as forgetting to do what others want, being sarcastic, withholding sex, gaining weight, and persisting in an annoying habit. Somehow or other, we find a way to make others pay for what they've done.

I am certainly a member of the passive-aggressive club. I see it most in my tendency to avoid relationships with those who tend to disagree the most with my values. Fortunately, I have no ability to tolerate things being not okay between me and those closest to me, which limits how far this might interfere with family and close friends.

It is almost impossible to avoid some level of withdrawal from relationship when one is resentful toward another person. Learning assertiveness is usually the best path to turn one's attention from passive-aggression to constructive expression of our feelings. When possible, this sometimes leads to immediate pay-offs, though at other times it may be one of those cases where things gets worse before they get better. A season of conflict may mark the beginning of a more assertive style, but there is no question that a greater level of connection, trust and intimacy will be made possible as a long-term result once the new communication style is accepted.

There is a danger, however, in making assertiveness sound like the easy solution to relational problems. In order to understand this, we have to take a step back and look at the big picture of power dynamics in a relationship. We all have many strategies for gaining power and control in relationships, from outright dominance to "playing the martyr," from overt financial status to manipulative game playing. If assertiveness simply becomes one more tool for the one who is "one up" in a relationship, the result will hardly be transformative.

When people feel like they're "one down" (the "losers" in their marriage or those near the bottom of the community pecking order), then the assertiveness of others can just feel like more evidence of their own failure. Consider the frustrated wife who after weeks of stewing in annoyance finally chooses to be assertive with her unemployed, video game-playing husband. We certainly feel sympathy for this woman, yet the result of her perfectly communicated assertiveness may well be that, internally, the husband simply agrees that he is a loser and feels more paralyzed than ever.

There are no instant answers to such relational complexities, regarding assertiveness or anything else. Assertiveness may be associated with confidence, but the relational impasse also requires the acceptance and communication of vulnerability and humility, even brokenness and messiness. That combination may be far too complex to script out in advance. This is one reason that some relational dilemmas are only resolved when a crisis shuffles the deck.

We don't generally seek such crises, but learning to tolerate the messiness of relationships helps us to be prepared and take advantage of the crises that will occur. Meanwhile, we can be determined to respect the needs of others and ourselves, hoping that the right balance of vulnerability, submission and assertiveness will help our stumbling journey toward a greater wholeness.

Empathy

As just mentioned, it is vital that the movement toward assertiveness, the risky process by which we strike out with others toward growth in trust, includes empathy if it is not to be self-centred and self-contained. In the latter part of the 20th century, empathy has become the central concept for understanding a healthy way of relating to another person.

There are many definitions available for empathy, but at its heart it is the ability to grasp the thoughts and feelings of another person with our own thoughts and feelings. In other words, it is not enough to be able to describe another's thoughts and feelings from a detached objective standpoint. Empathy also involves, to some extent, experiencing the other's thoughts and feelings as if they were our own (but without them actually becoming our own). There is always a one-foot-in and one-foot-out quality to healthy empathy—we don't lose ourselves within another person's perspective.

Empathy is nearly the opposite of dehumanizing, which was mentioned earlier. Generally, we empathize with those we see as sharing a common humanity with us. So, unless we are socially or psychologically damaged, we will usually attempt empathy with our immediate family, those we live with. Certainly we will do this with widely divergent degrees of success. For some personalities this will take great effort, while for others empathy will seem instinctive.

Recent discoveries of "mirror neurons" highlight that this ability to empathize is actually wired into our brains—certain nerve cells are automatically stimulated in ways that mimic what we see happening in others. To a certain extent we will actually feel another's pain and taste their sadness, frustration or joy. Of course, this automatic response does not necessarily lead to deep empathy, but when we add compassion plus a little imagination and communication, we have the ability to reach this deep understanding of another's experience, which is fully deserving of the word empathy.

The need for compassion, imagination and communication to round out empathy should not be minimized. Compassion is what motivates and grounds empathy in the good of the other, and imagination and communication emphasize that we need to be humble about the success of our empathic attempts. We can never know what is truly in the mind of another. From their words and a host of nonverbal cues, we can get significant insights, but there are many traps and blind spots, and much room for error.

Martin Buber, perhaps the greatest philosopher of communication, emphasizes that in spite of our best attempts at communication, there remains a gap between us and the true inner experience of another. We must make an "imaginative leap" in order to cross that gap and make our best guess as to what another is feeling and thinking. Then we use our own words and nonverbals to check out how close our imagination has come.

When counselling couples, I have come across many men who *are* actually attentive to and empathic (at least occasionally) with their wives, but whose wives don't realize this because the men have skipped the last step: they haven't shared their empathy and checked out how accurate it is. The wives are left unaware as to whether their husbands have understood, or if they still have their minds on work or when the ballgame starts.

Having started a look at empathy at the cellular level, with mirror neurons, we can follow a growing interest in what is happening all the way to the global level. Jeremy Rifkin, in *The Empathic Civilization,* describes an interesting history of the expansion of empathy. Millennia ago, humans were able to empathize among their blood ties (remember how early language development often identified one's tribe as the "people"). Outsiders were not people in the same way because empathy didn't reach that far. With developments in communication and transportation, this eventually extended to religious groups and then to nation states. We can empathize with those whose lives and struggles are important to us, those we identify as being like us. In spite of ongoing violence and ethnic strife, there are reasons for optimism that humanity is increasingly becoming able to consider the entire human race as being family—everyone is actually "like us," one of us, and therefore our empathy can extend globally. Rifkin considered the global response to the earthquake in Haiti as an example of this expanding empathy.

The obstacle to this growing circle of empathy is our human desire to resist empathizing when it is inconvenient. It is relatively easy to empathize with an earthquake victim; it is much harder to empathize with a victim of our own actions. It takes significant effort and moral courage to empathize with the parents of the children one's country has just killed while hunting terrorists. It takes above-average intentionality to empathize with the neighbours who are making noise when you are trying to sleep.

But it's when we most feel like resisting that empathy is most important for us to nurture.

Empathy plus

Empathy is one fundamental aspect of the way we connect with other human beings at our best. Yet in spite of this process seeming so deeply human, even empathy can become a fairly mechanical or even self-centred response. I can be accurately empathic even while the purpose of that empathy might be proving myself to be a good person, fulfilling the role expected of me, earning approval, or even using the empathic understanding I gain for my own ends. Empathy can be a performance that, for all its kindness or diligence, is still about myself. I can learn to master the skill of empathy without necessarily being authentically present in my relating to another.

While there is a fair consensus around the concept of empathy, things get less clear when we look for a deeper connection beyond empathy. One term, *attunement*, is gaining ground among those who study attachment theory: the understanding that we all develop a style of relating in our early years, based on both nature and nurture, that has a tendency to persist in our important relationships throughout our lives. These theorists suggest that an important part of the formation of secure attachment is a caregiver who is able to attune to his or her child. When attuned, two people seem dialled-in to the same frequency. They are each present, and they are each affected by the encounter. The baby's smile draws a genuine smile from the mother and a sparkle in her eye. The baby's cry brings a soothing concern.

Attunement meets a deep human need. Arguably, it is one of the most fundamental needs that we bring to a relationship. When someone is attuned to us, we experience a feeling of belonging, of mattering.

The opposite of attunement is either stonewalling or negation. Stonewalling involves completely shutting out the possibility of emotional engagement. In attachment studies, the opposite of attunement has been demonstrated with an experiment known as the still face experiment by Edward Tronick. This research powerfully demonstrated the negative effect on an infant when a caregiver remains impassive and unaffected by whatever it is the infant is doing to try to get attention. Negation is also a deeply troubling but surprisingly common experience when a person denies or rejects another's inner world. "No, there's nothing to be sad about," we too often say to upset children, denying their experience of disappointment. This causes deep confusion, shame and distrust of one's inner responses and emotions.

While the language of attunement is a little more mutual or reciprocal than empathy, the concepts still lie very close together. To stretch out even further, to add even more to empathy, we need to enter a territory where language gets mistier and often sounds idealistic.

Early in the 20th century, Martin Buber wrote a poetic, almost mystical, book called *I and Thou*.[3] While this small book has alternately deeply impressed or confused its readers, it remains one of the best expressions of the encounter that goes beyond what we normally think of as empathy. I suspect that Buber has chosen this poetic, indirect path to describe the type of connection at the heart in *I and Thou* because it needs to be understood intuitively. So my brief and direct summary will clearly fall far short of creating the heart encounter to which Buber is inviting his readers. But apart from advising those interested to pick up Buber's work, it is the best I can do.

The I-Thou relationship is one in which I am aware of mutual subjectivity—both I and the other are persons who think, feel and act in the world. The other has a whole world and a whole history within him or her that matters as much as my own. When we meet I am present and the other is present, and something new is created by the connection we share. I am present enough and vulnerable enough to be changed by this encounter. I feel myself releasing the self-centred agendas I may have as the connection of the moment becomes more important to me—in a sense, my self-

---

[3] Translated from the German, *Ich und Du*, contemporary English readers need to be aware of missing the connotation of "thou." This Old English word represents not formality and distance but closeness and intimacy.

centredness becomes external to me, bracketed, while my self-in-relationship has taken over my internal experience. Likewise the other is present to me, not as an object, not as someone I am performing a role for, but as a living, vulnerable and precious being who is being affected by his or her experience of me.

Idealistic language aside, we have all tasted these moments of connection, at least briefly. They may be intensely positive or quite difficult, but they will always be deeply meaningful moments. For some, the intimacy can be so unsettling that they scramble back for the cover of their detachment. If we do realize we need or want more of this kind of relating, we cannot simply choose to do this or script how such an encounter will happen. We prepare ourselves to be more available to such connections by practising our awareness of all others as equally and beautifully human, sharing a human world of thoughts, feelings, hopes and memories, in combinations as unique as snowflakes. Even brief encounters with supermarket cashiers or coffee shop servers can be chances to practise being more aware of this reality. Perhaps more challenging, we prepare ourselves for these moments by growing in trust toward ourselves and others, so that increasingly we can lay down the fears, self-consciousness, and need for control that normally insulate us from being fully present with another.

If normal empathy is closely watching or even conversing with someone on a dance floor, "empathy plus," attunement or an I-Thou encounter is entering the dance. Even with practise and decreasing insecurities, we can at best make ourselves available to such encounters, inviting others to truly meet us. The people around us will often not be able or willing to make themselves present, even when the invitation is there. Deep moments of connection will always remain occasional, rather than becoming the mode of all of our day-to-day relating. We may not often spend $30 or more for a bottle of good red wine, but what fine moments they are, when we can taste the good stuff with old or new friends.

Truth and the Other

Sometimes people wall themselves off from others because they see themselves as guardians of truth. We are at a time in popular culture when there is significant debate about the nature of truth. People who are seriously committed to faith traditions, modernist science or some political ideologies often feel that notions of absolute truth are central to what they believe. Yet in philosophical and scientific circles, notions of absolute truth have been seriously criticized for some time, and as these critiques are being popularized in the emerging postmodern culture of our day, we see a kickback. Postmodern ideas, on the other hand, seem to have led to confusion and a lack of confidence that has sapped some individuals and groups of their energy and motivation. People need confidence in order to act decisively, and some have felt their confidence deeply shaken by the fragmented and contradictory understandings of truth to which we are now exposed.

In response to the postmodern or multicultural threat, some have named Absolute Truth as the hill on which to take a stand. I would suggest that it is the very combative nature inherent in the language of absolute truth that makes it so problematic. The concept of absolute truth is of no use to those who are humbly aware that even if a final, absolute understanding of truth somehow exists, none of us have a perfect grasp of this purity. Most of us would agree that if there is an absolute truth, experientially we are talking about a truth we are reaching toward but have not yet attained.

Similarly, nearly everyone would agree that we are at least capable of moving in the direction of better truth. Communities discern and individuals grow in their understanding of the world. Therefore, the vast majority of us, even most of those sympathetic to postmodern ideas, are experientially (if not theoretically) critical relativists: we understand that we are capable, and hopefully choose, to move in the direction of what is truer, while acknowledging that we have not yet arrived at the destination of truth. Annoyingly, most abstract arguments about truth take place in the extreme margins as if this large common ground did not exist.

For me, then, the question is a relational one. How will I speak of truth with another? How will my understanding of truth affect the way that I relate to someone else whose understandings of truth differ from mine? If I refer to something as absolute truth when discussing with someone who disagrees, I disrespect the other person and negate any opportunity for genuine dialogue. The adjective "absolute" only communicates exclusion—of ideas and people.

I once tried to share this perspective on truth with a well-known Christian ministry, which was distributing videos aimed at correcting those who failed to believe that there was a "universal standard of absolute truth." The reply to my email suggested, "You can't be a Christian at all if you don't believe that [some things are still black and white]." When I continued the conversation by telling them that their suggestion that I wasn't, in fact, a Christian was hardly a respectful way to carry on a dialogue, I received another reply, which stated their "final word on the subject," apparently missing the irony that they were now proving my point by first disrespecting me and then refusing dialogue.

It seems that many people seem to miss what their own emphasis on absolutes and certainty communicates to those who disagree. How can there be respectful dialogue with someone who, whether politely or rudely, insists that they are absolutely right and the other is, therefore, absolutely wrong?

Of course, at the beginning of a dialogue, if I have any confidence at all, I start by believing that my current understanding is the best one. Here there is no disrespect, and genuine dialogue can proceed, creating the possibility of shifting understandings in one or both parties.

What we do need is confidence. It's painful to see the indecision and aimlessness that characterizes many of those affected by postmodern thinking or by the confusion of a shifting, pluralistic world. Confidence, however, does not require certainty. I am reasonably confident that I will arrive at my destination when I fly, and so I board an airplane in spite of no certainty about the character of my pilot or the perfect maintenance of the airplane.

There are many understandings of the nature of truth. Personally, I find narrative understandings very helpful. Narrative truth implies that we understand the world well when we are able to tell stories that make good sense out of our experience. These stories give us confidence to engage and act decisively in our world, even while we know that paradoxically, contrary stories might also make good sense of another's experience. Still other stories become "thin" stories that are so bound and constricted in their understandings that they take away people's ability to make their way through their world with freedom and growth. By telling more open-ended, "thicker" stories, we can invite others to consider new ways to narrate their lives and to explore the real possibilities that are available. Narrative understandings of truth are rich and flexible, yet well able to empower individuals and groups even in the midst of a fragmented culture. My first counselling supervisor once told me that counsellors need "a soft bosom and a firm backbone." I find that this is exactly what a narrative understanding of truth invites. Narrative truth allows personal confidence combined with deep and respectful engagement with others who story their lives differently.

The will to embrace and the will to purity

Instead of moving toward truth in mutual conversations with those both similar and different from us, the human tendency has been to use truth to exclude others from the conversation. When this happens, so-called "truth" divides and dehumanizes instead of drawing us together toward fruitful understanding. This tendency toward exclusion of others, sometimes obvious and sometimes subtle, has nowhere been so clearly described as in the brilliant work of Miroslav Volf in his book, *Exclusion and Embrace*. Raised in the conflict-torn Balkans, Volf is able to bring depth and reality to an exploration of our call to embrace even the enemies who have done great harm to us or our loved ones.

Volf's book is a thoughtful and personal response to the cycles of violence that he experienced openly in Croatia and more systemically in quieter parts of the world. His analysis points out that when we try to assimilate those who are different, we are still practising exclusion by trying to destroy the aspects of others that are different from us. But by maintaining a paradoxical combination of distance and identity from our own cultures and communities, we can create a space that enables us to open our arms with a "will to embrace" the other.

Despite how deeply I was touched by reading Volf's book, I needed another set of lenses to bring his message into clear focus. This was provided by psychologist (and theologian) Richard Beck, who wrote the book, *Unclean*. This book drives home the significance of our need to ensure that the "will to embrace" precedes the "will to purity." It is far too typical of many of us, and perhaps even more so of our communities and traditions, to flip that around. We are usually willing to consider embracing as long as it doesn't disturb our ability to protect our purity.

Beck uses his insight into the "psychology of disgust" to clarify the problems that are created by our responses to otherness. When concerns about purity trump our commitment to embrace, the natural effect is to feel and communicate disgust toward those who we consider might contaminate us or our communities. This is why the apparent wisdom in "loving the sinner but hating the sin" does not work out experientially, as the gay community has been trying to tell Christians for a long time (setting aside the question of whether or not homosexual behaviour is sinful). When we try to hold loving the sinner and hating the sin as parallel truths, they tend not to stay equal. The disgust (and political heat) created by hating the sin too often trumps the personal reality of loving the sinner. How, for example, does a pastor successfully communicate love to someone whose identity is closely bound up with a practice the pastor considers hateful and disgusting?

On a more violent level, consider the dehumanization necessary for us to tolerate the predictable death of civilians when we start bombing a foreign country. Is it our tendency to emphasize purity that makes it possible to ignore the deaths of civilians when they are associated with a faith or political ideology that we feel must be rejected? If, perhaps below the surface, we are disgusted by the (violent, fundamentalist, and/or primitive) beliefs of other people, we are much more likely to minimize the seriousness of such "collateral damage." "It's not like these are civilized people," we almost seem to be saying to ourselves, though not usually out loud because that would expose our hypocrisy. In fact, most of the dehumanizing strategies mentioned earlier in this chapter seem to go hand-in-hand with an emphasis on purity.

The alternative to exclusion, to an emphasis on purity, is genuinely risky—do we really open our arms with a will to embrace the other? What about the risks to our safety? What if values we hold dear are challenged or undermined? When the will to embrace becomes far more important than the will to purity, there will be sacrifices. I wonder if, on a deeper level, some of the purity we are longing for might only come through choosing such sacrifices?

Getting Practical

Read a book representing the Other. If you like reading non-fiction works, find an author with a point of view quite different from your own on a subject you care about. Set aside your judgment of the author's opinion until you deeply consider the value and bits of truth that you find within it. Don't let yourself argue against it until you understand what convinced the author to form his or her point of view. When you have managed to find at least some aspects of the work to appreciate, consider how this perspective might nuance your own views. If you like fiction, choose a good novel with a main character that you do not find particularly likeable, and then read it empathically, as if this character were someone coming into your life that you have a chance to befriend.

Develop new perspectives on friends and family. Think of people near to you that you have trouble appreciating at the moment. How can you see them with fresh eyes? Imagine that you see them through the eyes of someone able to see more positively than you—perhaps even pray to see that person through God's eyes. Consider questions like: What is delightful or unique about this person? What bothers me about this person and why does it bother me? Does my "concern" for him or her cloak a fear of my own? What is there about me that might trouble this person? Are there ways in which we're different that I deny or disrespect? What if I accepted those differences as something invigorating and dynamic?

Look for missed opportunities for friendship/hospitality. Consider some possibilities for developing a new friendship. Or, together with your family, explore possibilities of people that you might show hospitality toward that you have resisted acting on because there is something about them that makes you somehow uncomfortable.

Purge the myth of redemptive violence. Walter Wink describes how pervasive our training is in the "myth of redemptive violence." He writes:

> The belief that violence "saves" is so successful because it doesn't seem to be mythic in the least. Violence simply appears to be the nature of things. It's what works. It seems inevitable, the last and, often, the first resort in conflicts. If a god is what you turn to when all else fails, violence certainly functions as a god. What people overlook, then, is the religious character of violence. It demands from its devotees an absolute obedience-unto-death.
>
> This myth of redemptive violence is the real myth of the modern world. It, and not Judaism or Christianity or Islam, is the dominant religion in our society today.

One of the things that convinced Wink that this mythic structure is so entirely pervasive in our culture was the fact that it formed the structure of nearly all children's cartoons. Heroes and villains struggle until the moment when the hero finally (but, of course, only temporarily) vanquishes his foes. The next few movies you watch (or books that you read), look for the presence of the myth of redemptive violence. What really saves the day in the end—forgiveness, reconciliation and embrace? Or the domination of the sword?

6 JOURNEYING TOGETHER

There is a beautiful story of a young man with a disability who wanted to win the Special Olympics; he got to the 100-metre race and he was running like crazy to get that gold medal. One of the others running with him slipped and fell; he turned round and picked him up and they ran across the finish line together last. Are we prepared to sacrifice the prize for solidarity? It's a big question. Do we want to win or do we want to be in solidarity with others?

– Jean Vanier

We need a moral prophetic minority of all colors who muster the courage to question the powers that be, the courage to be impatient with evil and patient with people, and the courage to fight for social justice. In many instances we will be stepping out on nothing, hoping to land on something.

– Cornel West

Imagine a sociologist who has outgrown a fundamentalist upbringing. Her two boys are in high school, and she has struggled to raise them, largely on her own after a messy divorce. She wants to be proud of them, but their days seem to be filled with video games and isolated hours on their laptops. Their arguments about so many things seem to end up with her being stymied by an inability to convince them of a better way.

One day, as part of a research project, a colleague gets her an invitation to share supper with an Amish family in rural Pennsylvania. During the first half of the evening, her appreciation of their warm welcome, the chicken soup with broad noodles and the fresh homemade bread, is eclipsed by the inner judgments that she feels toward the backwardness of their rigid gender roles. In her mind, the relatively silent children are proof that their children are taught to be "seen and not heard." When they are made to stay at the table for a lengthy Bible reading after the meal, she is sure that they are pointlessly stuck in a different century.

Then, as things get more relaxed after the meal, they talk about the priorities of their community and how they have accepted some technology while rejecting much. She is surprised by their thoughtful understanding of what their communities have gained through these sacrifices and boundaries. Then her feelings toward the family change completely when they describe their response to a mass shooting in which an outsider murdered five Amish schoolgirls before killing himself. In response to her questions, they describe their beliefs and the understandings that led them to feel that it was only natural to forgive the man and to offer immediate forgiveness and comfort to the murderer's family.

They tell her the story of Dirk Willems, passed on for hundreds of years, who, while literally running for his life because of religious persecution, stopped to rescue his pursuer when he fell through the ice. As a result Willems was captured, tortured and killed, but remembered as a hero because he acted with the love of God. In a similar way, they tell her that of course God had given them the strength to respond to their devastation and pain with compassion and forgiveness. They still find themselves confused, though, why "the English" made such a big deal of this response.

Driving home, she is surprised at the longing she feels deep within her. She doesn't want to become Amish, to forsake her freedoms and her education. But she feels acutely aware of her lack of stories to guide her teen boys, and her lack of community to back her up in her lonely struggle to raise them well. The Amish family's reasons for doing what they did were concrete, heartfelt and shared. The rationales she struggled to communicate to her boys always ended up sounding dry and abstract. She knew she needed to get more intentional about finding others to journey with if she wanted to find a better way.

~

Communities, like the Amish, that seem so intentional about the kind of lives they want to live are somewhat of a paradox. In one way they set a strong example for us, while at the same time their rigidity and sense of exclusion and separation prevent their example from having much of an effect on the larger society. I've just suggested in the last chapter that wholeness is based far more on a will to embrace than a will to purity. But are embracing, open-minded communities and individuals left with no moral compass, with an "anything goes" approach?

I would like to suggest that taking the risks and even making the sacrifices required by a universal willingness to embrace others in spite of their differences from us actually puts us in a position where the goals originally behind purity and certainty find new life. Perhaps this would become clearer if we explore possibilities regarding where such a journey together could lead.

Most of us realize, albeit sometimes with desperation, that we must seek a more whole way to live together. The Hebrew word *shalom* (and similarly the Arabic *salaam* and other related words) is a glorious ancient word for this vision of a better way to live life together. It is a word for peace that is set in a context of a community in harmony with creation, living justly with each other.

It is the peace of individuals with integrity and faithfulness, experiencing relative prosperity and physical health.

One of my favourite metaphors for this vision of shalom is the banquet table—the diverse, sumptuous feast where all are invited. Anyone who has helped prepare a feast knows that this kind of celebration does not just happen. It is not a spontaneous result of "anything goes." It comes about as people commit themselves, roll up their sleeves and work together to make a vision happen. Agreements and compromises need to be "put on the menu," which is probably at its best when including recipes based on tradition and personal creativity. The best ingredients are home grown or gathered as a result of sustainable, good work. And a final key to a feast's success is knowing how to throw the doors open and invite all who are willing to come and join in. Moral laziness will not create this kind of banquet, but the stories and laughter, songs and tears, will make all of the sacrifice and effort worthwhile, even when the "banquet" is just sampled in a piece of bread shared between friends.

So, the invitation to journey together is a call for individuals and communities to create this kind of banquet. It is a pursuit of ways of living that are just and hopeful and peaceful, because they seek to make the celebration of creation, of life, available to all people. It is a rhythm that involves understanding and removing the obstacles to inclusive celebration—obstacles in ourselves and in our communities—and then the deliberate inviting of all to share the banquet with us.

This may seem idealistic. But when our ever-present human weaknesses of fear and laziness make us give in to individual and corporate self-centredness, greed, competition, exclusion and violence, we have often been saved from despair by those who dared to be idealistic, successfully communicating their invitation to a better way. The visions of historic figures, like Moses, Jesus, Mohammed and Buddha are celebrated and remembered through major religious traditions that have endured many centuries. Closer to our times, we have seen more life-sized examples that demonstrate that these invitations keep coming. We see this in the new life breathed into the ways of nonviolence by Gandhi and

Martin Luther King Jr. We've seen Mother Teresa's example of selfless care for "the poorest of the poor." Jean Vanier showed us a more humane way to care for the intellectually and developmentally disabled through the creation of L'Arche communities. In South Africa, Nelson Mandela and Desmond Tutu showed us that structures of evil and violence could be replaced with a struggling pathway toward forgiveness and reconciliation.

Perhaps even more plentiful are the groups that keep demonstrating that life can be lived differently. One classic example is the Koinonia community in Georgia. Risking their lives, they created an interracial community dedicated to peace, and among the fruit of this long-standing community has been the birth of Habitat for Humanity. In 1989 and 1990 there was the sudden burst of (primarily) nonviolent protests that helped put an end to the Iron Curtain, most symbolically with the destruction of the Berlin Wall. Spanning the turn of the millennium, there were the women of Liberia—Christians and Muslims—who came together singing, praying and protesting, helping to end years of bloodshed and paving the way for the election of the first woman president in Africa.

These individuals and groups have done more than show us a vision of wholeness—they have demonstrated that it is possible. We can learn to live together in ways that lead to healing, justice and peace. A desire to embrace the Other, to de-emphasize dogmatic or ideological purity and certainty, enable this movement toward shalom, rather than limiting it.

Solidarity

With accurate perception, we do not need to choose a stance of solidarity, but simply recognize the truth of it. We are all poor and weak and powerless, dependent on each other and on a healthy planet.

This is harder to see when we are blinded by those things that we use to insulate us from facing the pain of our poverty, weakness and impotence. So we hoard things, get addicted to pleasures, build up bank accounts and mutual funds, accumulate influence and power. For many of us, we only admit that we aren't actually in control of our destiny or our happiness during those rare moments when some crisis forces us to see the impotence beyond our pretences of power.

When we can begin to admit our own poverty, we are then in a position to recognize the truth in those famously paradoxical "beatitudes" of Jesus, beginning with "blessed are the poor." We are setting out on the right path when we realize that we share the experience of human need and limitation. Seeing our solidarity allows us to choose solidarity not out of pity or charity (which, of course, is not real solidarity at all) but out of sincere recognition of what we have in common.

Solidarity is the starting place for our journey for two reasons: 1) we begin authentically, with the awareness of our own need for healing and growth, and our own need for relationship, and 2) our invitation is freed from condescension and the imposition of power. Most of us are not really looking for intrusive peddlers of religion or ideology. Imagine the difference if, instead of a tract-pusher, someone came to your door and said, "I'm interested in chatting with people about what helps them cope with the challenges of the world these days. Are you interested in sharing what works or doesn't work for you?" We still may not like the intrusion or the leap into intimacy, but wouldn't it be a breath of fresh air (if it were honest)?

So much of our attempt to "help" is tainted by hypocrisy and condescension. We pretend we're happier or more healed than we are, or we reach down from the heights as if we had certain answers or all the best stuff. Then we're offended when those we try to help are less than responsive, and we use their lacklustre response to prove that "they don't want to be helped." It's so much easier to receive help from those who genuinely see themselves to be "like us." We're not generous philanthropists passing out free tickets to the undeserving; we're sharing the news that we all belong at the table.

Change and suffering: Turning back to find the right road

For Buddhists, a foundational teaching is that life is suffering. We may or may not agree that suffering is quite that omnipresent, but we certainly all know the experience of suffering. And we have all experienced that suffering has sometimes been crucial in helping us choose better paths, or has simply been a required part of the process of dismantling an unhelpful life pattern in order to begin rebuilding a better one, individually or corporately.

I hate having to turn back. When I'm driving down the road and realize I've forgotten something or missed an exit or simply taken the wrong road, I really hate the pain of having to turn around, wasting the past few minutes and knowing (in that present state of mind) that I am required to waste the next precious minutes of my life by turning around.

Of course, it's never really wasting time to get back on the right path. But the whole time that I'm going "backwards" I cause myself mental anguish through my resistance to accepting the reality of my mistake and the effort required to correct it. Even that moment of realizing the truth, important and helpful though it may be, is experienced as painful.

Most of us resist change. Often it feels just like that necessity of turning back, of undoing something. We feel the shame of exposing a mistake or the weight of the extra effort required. Sometimes we are so resistant that we desperately pretend there is another way. Can I do without what I forgot? Maybe this wrong road will still get me where I need to go? Can't I somehow just ignore the mistake?

Since we all know this pain, we are sometimes kind but unhelpful to each other. We provide untimely reassurance, enabling someone to keep driving down the wrong road instead of facing the pain of turning around: "It's not that bad." "Things will get better." In the doomed days of a crumbling society about to fall to an aggressive empire, the Hebrew prophet, Jeremiah, tried to help his people face the necessity of suffering in order to change. His words were unheeded because it was easier for everyone to listen to those giving false reassurance, "saying, 'Peace, peace', when there is no peace" (Jer.6.14). It is so much harder for us to help people toward honesty and courage. It means feeling pain and staying with people in their pain.

Anthropologists have named a fundamental pattern in the way people have come to help each other to change, a pattern seen in rites of passage and of healing rituals throughout the world. This pattern involves three steps: 1) leaving normal, 2) time in a liminal or marginal space, and 3) reincorporation. One of the benefits of naming this pattern is to gain a deeper appreciation of the middle step.

We understand the pain of turning around: we realize that when our "normal" sucks, we have to change. But sometimes we forget that we can't immediately dive into a better life on the right road. The word "liminal" is related to the word "limbo." It's an in-between space; it's the wilderness. And very often we need to spend some time in this in-between space before we get to the place where we can really start on the better path. The liminal space is the time in our life when we might be grieving the old, the familiar—what we left behind even if we knew it wasn't working for us. This is especially true because of that sense of going backwards. We're not yet seeing the fruit of a better life. So, like the wilderness, it feels empty and barren. It takes great maturity or support to really trust that this empty, liminal space is the pathway to life. A genuine awareness of the old suffering, the honest confidence that it had definitely been the wrong road that we had been on, then becomes our friend in helping us make it through.

Of course, change is not *always* difficult. Sometimes a deep change, like the kind we might call a conversion, can be accompanied with great enthusiasm. The promise of the new, perhaps combined with being thoroughly "done" with the old, makes us ready without hesitation to embrace a transformation. A liminal time may still follow. The enthusiasm starts to wane, or the realization that our transformed lives are hardly perfect makes us wonder how many conversions still lie ahead.

Language, community and making sense of life

Before the 20th century, moving toward change or healing was largely shaped by the understandings of a community. Elders or healers helped people to know when and how it was time to leave the old normal. Time in a liminal space was understood and supported, and most importantly, everyone knew that a welcome back to community, of the person somehow changed, was the final step.

One of the most important things a community does for its members is to provide the tools required to make sense of life. These tools are effective when they provide a relatively common understanding. So language, rituals, traditions and everyday practices are all infused with meanings that are more or less shared among the members. Words give names and allow conversation; they become the building blocks of stories and songs. Shared practices map out possible trails through the terrain of life. Out of the chaos, we start to see patterns and meaning emerge. We become a part of the ongoing stories, and we shape their outcome.

The value of these shared tools can break down, however. Agreement on meaning can fall apart. Factions and power imbalances within communities can tempt those in authority into harnessing language and ritual in order to dominate and control the rest of the community or society. Then seeds of new language and new traditions rise up among the marginalized, giving new potential meanings but breaking down the commonality. The imperial dominance of the Tower of Babel becomes dispersed by the diversity of new languages and subcultures.

We live in an era in which our Tower of Babel is being built by corporations. The dominant empire is one that teaches us the language of individualism and consumerism. This language encourages us to understand that our needs can be met by products and that meaning can be found in services that we shop for. Psychotherapists become our secular priests and talk shows provide our gurus. Our Babel teaches us to accept the supposedly deserved hierarchy that separates those with mutual funds and bonuses from those earning minimum wage or even more minimal welfare cheques. Competition replaces cooperation as the ground for social behaviour. Stories, myth, art or even more likely, professional sports, are available as purchased entertainment to divert us from clearly seeing the life-sucking Tower that we are all building.

The countercultural emphasis on local communities versus grandiosity is part of the needed subversion and diversity. We need to remember the old deep stories and myths that have warned us of the tragic danger of the hubris of humanity—stories like the Tower of Babel, or the Icarus myth. Stories, including the language that makes them possible and the rituals that help us experience and recall them, are the ground of our resistance to meaninglessness or oppressive empire. One of the most profound conclusions in 20th century ethics was that of Alasdair MacIntyre, who, in *After Virtue,* wrote, "I can only answer the question, 'What am I to do?' if I can answer the prior question 'Of what story or stories do I find myself a part?'.... Mythology, in its original sense, is at the heart of things."

This creates a dilemma because it seems that competitive rationalism and consumer-driven science have forced our remembered symbols, stories and traditions into a mill that grinds out either an indefensible literalism among those desperately holding on to past understandings, or a sterile scepticism among those letting go. Preserving the life-giving metaphors and meanings in which these traditions are rooted is very difficult and will be continually challenged on both sides.

Some would try to preserve this meaning in metaphorical (or sometimes literal) museums—quaint reminders of where past generations have found the best meaning they could in their limited ways. But museums are not living communities. Stories and traditions need to be lived out together; a language needs to be preserved in active speech and shared rituals that change people's lives.

The difficulty we have in challenging our Tower of Babel with the stories of a living community is perhaps best seen in the recent wave of atheism in western nations. It's easy to respect atheists who have thoughtfully grappled with the damage that has been done by badly lived religion and have honestly come to the conclusion that belief in God—any God—is dangerous and unhelpful. But considering how mysterious and indefinable God is, I can't help but wonder if some modern atheism also represents a lack of imagination. If we have no way left to speak about, tell stories about, and orient our lives around a mysterious Centre of life, then I don't understand where one finds the ground on which to stand. Is there still some source of reverence that helps us understand and experience our smallness while being in awe at the possibility and beauty of something much bigger than ourselves? Is there a foundation broad enough to enable resistance against the pressures of mass culture or the tyranny of one's own ego? The pressures are huge, twisting weak understandings of God and ultimate commitments into the service of corporate profit or political ideology. Our egos so readily deceive us into thinking that self-protection and self-centredness are good and necessary. A strong commitment to something broad and inclusive, deeply rooted, flexible and empathic is needed to give us the freedom to resist these forces. Perhaps, though, it is my own lack of imagination that prevents me from understanding that atheists can find that foundation in some other direction.

Personally, I have found pursuit of an understanding of God and a commitment to attempting to love God more than myself to be my solid ground. Love of God has inspired me to pursue the depths of my own Christian tradition and given me the courage to be open to the best ideas and beauty in other traditions. My understandings of God have changed often enough to know that my present conclusions are still very flawed and limited, but they seem to be getting more life giving. A life with God has, at least somewhat, helped limit my self-centredness and given me hope to believe in the depth of meaning and love in the face of opposing forces. And, perhaps best of all, an orientation toward God has been a key to creating the formation of communities that enabled all of this to be a shared journey.

It is not surprising that there is a great hunger for community in our present society. This is a great challenge because in spite of this hunger, we have been trained to be wary of commitment.

People want community but want full individual freedoms and rights as well. This is not an impossible tension, but it is a paradoxical one. Not everyone can trust that we gain true freedom only through commitments, that we gain our lives by losing them.

When communities have thrived in our modern and postmodern age, they are usually based on a combination of rootedness and fresh interpretation. They have looked for language that connects with the best of tradition while breaking free from the dead ends to which some paths have led. Marginalizing and oppressing traditions, in particular, are increasingly being abandoned or reinterpreted. Tired rituals have been creatively adapted until they come alive.

In my community, one of the best examples of this is in the Celtic liturgical service that some of us developed as an experiment a few years ago. Seeking an alternative service that was contemplative and simple, we pieced together a "morning prayer," borrowing bits from other communities and the Bible, and adding these to some original writing. As in the Celtic tradition, we wanted the liturgy to be embodied, practical and honouring of the natural world. We wanted the affirmations to be grounded in tradition, including a centring on the "breaking of bread," and we wanted our little group to be connected with the larger, global church through the reading of the *Revised Common Lectionary* to which we also add a contemporary reading in order to remember that God continues to speak through poets and writers from a variety of traditions.

Coming from a non-liturgical tradition myself, I was surprised as the weeks went by how the service grew to be so deeply meaningful to me. It became a place to connect with others, close friends or newcomers, as we shared reflections on how the readings struck us or as individuals offered short, heartfelt prayers to which we all responded, "Hear our prayer." On a 40-minute journey, it feels as though we enter a holy place together, experience confession and forgiveness, and emerge renewed and reoriented. The familiar words of the liturgy continue to both challenge and encourage me in a way that affects the direction of my life. The context of the service—preceded by coffee and muffins and followed by lingering chat around café tables—keeps the tone informal and friendly.

As a therapist, I am very aware of how many people don't have access to that kind of weekly renewal among friends. They have no tools to let go of the remorse they feel over their mistakes. They have no point of connection to ancient truths and no one who will back up the cry of their heart by saying, "Hear our prayer." They have few signposts other than the latest entertainment-oriented talk show authors to guide the direction of their life. Communities that provide a meaningful pattern and language are crucial, but we must seek them out and commit to them in order to experience the life-giving result.

Naming evil

One of the casualties of the breakdown of community is the diluted and powerless language that much of society has settled for in naming the very serious obstacles to wholeness. In our therapeutic culture there are plenty of guides to point out all the obstacles to mental, relational and physical health that exist, many of which are probably quite helpful. Somehow, though, in all the self-help books and talk shows, the whole process has seemed to become very prosaic and consumeristic—as if the point of it all is mere self-improvement.

I once attended a very stimulating seminar on a therapeutic approach taught by an enthusiastic therapist. The orientation was so focused on the positive that our guide kept insisting, "we all do the best we can with what we have." In private conversations, I pushed him on how deeply he meant this, and found that he was completely immersed in an outlook in which there was no evil and no sin. He genuinely believed that we all, always, choose the best thing with the personal resources we have at hand. Forgiveness was never required, only gracious understanding.

While feeling that there was something compelling about this point of view, which so strongly avoids blame and judgment, I could not accept it. I was too aware of personal choices that I had made in spite of plentiful resources that could have enabled me to choose better. Along with all the human family, I am often willing, at some level intentionally, to choose real pain for others in order to protect myself. I find it helpful to call that human tendency evil, especially when these choices are covered up or justified even though we are given an opportunity to face them and change.

Sometimes the watered-down nature of therapeutic, self-help language makes me wonder about what has been lost, even with the old language of evil and the devil. The trouble is that those who most use these terms today are often seen by society as antiquated and judgmental, and, at least some of the time, society would probably be right in that assessment. When these powerful terms are used too literally and too much in the service of judgment and exclusion, we are right to be wary. They are dangerous words and should be used with caution, impassioned only with sincere love and with much care to avoid self-righteousness.

As Scott Peck writes in *People of the Lie*, it's especially important to face and name the evil part of human nature when it gets particularly resistant to the light of day. There is little to be gained by cranking up the language—naming evil—when speaking of careless selfishness or even a momentary act of malice prompted by a flash of hurt and anger. But we need strong language to wake us up to the damaging reality of the kind of evil that crushes hearts, families, and societies while cloaking itself as necessary or good. It's evil when people abuse their children and resist the help that could enable them to stop. It's evil when we intentionally maintain structures that exploit the weak for the benefit of those with power and wealth.

Perhaps even here our red flags go up. Are we not in danger of slipping back into exclusion when we start naming evil in this way? Will this block us from inviting the pedophile or the narcissistic CEO into healing community and the possibility of change?

For me, a crucial prerequisite for the value of naming evil is that we recognize its presence inside each of us. This may have been most clearly stated by Alexander Solzhenitsyn, who, in *The Gulag Archipelago*, wrote:

If only there were evil people somewhere insidiously committing evil deeds, and it were necessary only to separate them from the rest of us and destroy them. But the line dividing good and evil cuts through the heart of every human being. And who is willing to destroy a piece of his own heart?

This is not to say that evil is only personal or individual. Evil also takes root within structures and institutions. A classic exposition of this would be Walter Wink's, *The Powers that Be*. In this excellent summary of his trilogy on "the powers," Wink names the powers as the "angels" of any particular group or organization. These powers have often fallen into self-serving "domination systems" and their perpetuation has been maintained by the "myth of redemptive violence." This myth has been so pervasive that it transforms those who fight against the fallen powers into servants of similar domination systems—those who fight evil often become evil in the process (as Nietzsche said about fighting monsters). Of course another side of evil involves passively allowing these systems to dominate without any resistance at all.

Wink sees the way to fight evil in the actively resistant but nonviolent "third way," a path taught and practised by the likes of Jesus, Gandhi and Martin Luther King. In other words, we can redeem the powers when we resist with love and respect those who have been caught up in dehumanizing domination systems, though this might sometimes cost us our lives.

Those who see evil as residing largely in such structural evil have mostly chosen to fight evil by becoming advocates of social justice. Yet in the midst of all the activism, it becomes possible to lose sight of Solzhenitsyn's insight. Personal evil and structural evil are not either/or choices. All those who have struggled for social justice over the long haul have had to learn the contemplative work or spiritual empowerment that is required to sustain such a long and difficult battle without becoming part of the problem. We must change human hearts and not just human systems in order to overcome evil.

Likewise, those who have overemphasized that changing the individual human heart must come first may have forgotten that social justice doesn't spontaneously arise through individual goodness. Evil woven into social structures knows only too well how to hide and cover itself up. Some of the most profound words that I've read this past decade were in an open letter from a South African, Peter Storey, writing to North Americans in the wake of 9/11:

> You have to expose, and confront, the great disconnect between the kindness, compassion and caring of most American people, and the ruthless way American power is experienced, directly and indirectly, by the poor of the earth. *You have to help good people see how they have let their institutions do their sinning for them.* This is not easy among people who really believe that their country does nothing but good, but it is necessary, not only for their future, but for us all. *(Italics mine)*

If Solzhenitsyn is right that the "line dividing good and evil cuts through the heart of every human being" then we do no one a favour by watering down our language about the serious obstacles we face in seeking wholeness. Evil at all levels must be named and faced, beginning with ourselves and the structures that we all make possible.

Providing signposts, pathways and boundaries

While earlier I've emphasized Volf's point that the "will to embrace" must precede the "will to purity," the pervasiveness of evil means we all need help in understanding limits. Healthy communities guide individuals by embodying ethical pathways through the complexities of life. Hopefully these pathways are flexible and maintained with grace and forgiveness—those who stray, wander or test out new paths are not rejected, ostracized or marginalized. But it should matter when there is significant deviation from ethical pathways. Sometimes that "mattering" might mean a community shifts its expectations or provides needed support and encouragement. Sometimes, it just means that a lively and respectful discussion is opened up.

Communities can be magnifiers of the ethical trajectories or intentions—good or bad—of their individual members. Groups of people with especially broken, fearful and/or lazy members are capable of much greater evil than any of their individuals members alone. Scott Peck's study of this dynamic in *People of the Lie*, based on his analysis of the atrocities committed in My Lai, Vietnam, provides excellent insight into this process. On the other hand, communities (still filled with broken people) can embody a way of life far more graced than what is possible by most individuals on their own.

Groups that shine in this way are able to do this because individual failures, weaknesses and shortcomings are assumed to be a part of the reality of living out the ideals. A community can support the vision of marriage as a lifelong union that is not lightly severed, but this does not mean that divorce never occurs within such a community, nor need it mean that those who find divorce to be a necessary option are marginalized by their choices.

The success of managing this tension is certainly not to be taken for granted, nor does it come easily. It is very challenging to communicate an inspiring vision while not communicating judgment of those who have visibly fallen short of that vision. In fact, in terms of communication alone, it may be impossible. We accept that we will never live up to our own or our community's ideals, even while the community stumbles forward in embodying them. We accept that diversity within and around the community will mean the vision is constantly questioned and often transformed as we learn from mistakes.

As difficult a tension this is, communities do sometimes manage it. There have been many communities in my life that have created contexts that have shaped my character, attitudes and behaviour by representing ways of life that reached for a higher vision than the surrounding society. In churches, school communities and other contexts, I have been surrounded by people who have expected and encouraged better behaviour. Self-centred greed, disrespect of others and destructive lifestyle decisions would not have felt at home in these settings, and I am much the better for it. Yet, in most cases, this ethical encouragement has not happened through a pressure to perform in order to win acceptance (though no doubt there have been many exceptions). And, I expect, my personality has made me less sensitive than others might be to some of the less-than-graceful social expectations that might have been present in my communities.

Just this past week, I became frustrated at a small group of people in my church for, in my perception, having carelessly interfered with something I was involved in, and not for the first time. I spoke to them with visible frustration and annoyance and marched off. That happened prior to a church service. Before I left church that day, mostly without my initiation, every person involved had individually spoken to me, and we had all mutually apologized and cleared the air. I was delighted to be a part of a group that was not okay with walking away from each other with bad feelings unaddressed. Of course, this is not true every day.

When communities do manage to pull this off and find the right balance, something amazing becomes possible. Outsiders visit and experience a unique flavour that makes them want to live better. Previous settings that did not provide this kind of context are exposed as being too careless and carefree to bring out the best in us, too judgmental to allow authenticity or diversity, or simply too fragmented and alienated to even notice what anybody else does.

The wounded healer: Safety, pain and healing

Another important way in which communities help enable individuals on this journey together is to provide opportunities for healing. Whether through structural evil, ordinary circumstances, the bad choices of friends and family, or our own poor decisions, we all end up wounded in many ways. This means that solidarity on the journey together is the foundation for helping each other to heal. One of the best expressions of this is found in Henri Nouwen's book, *The Wounded Healer*. While many have read this short, classic work, many more have simply affirmed the truth of the term, which psychologist Carl Jung names as an archetype. We don't invite others to walk with us toward wholeness because we have already arrived, but because we all share the woundedness that is a part of being human. We've all been hurt and we've all done the hurting. In Nouwen's words it means there is "a constant willingness to see one's own pain and suffering as rising from the depth of the human condition which all [people] share."

The "wounded healer" concept does not mean we are all helpless and hopeless, lost in a sea of brokenness. It means that from a position of solidarity and care, we share the sources and possibilities of healing with each other. The caring relationship itself is the most notable source of healing.

In the midst of reading about what actually happens in the brain when people are healed in psychotherapy, I came across what psychologist Louis Cozolino suggests is the common factor behind virtually all therapies: the creation of a "safe emergency." He describes many psychological wounds as resulting from the mind's inability to cope with the emotions of a troubling experience. As a result, the experience is never processed and integrated—it's never "made sense of" or woven into the coherent narratives of our lives. The emotions embedded in the memory remain raw and threatening; we avoid thinking about the unhealed memory, but it is like undigested food that sits too long in the stomach, causing unease and disease.

What we need in order to heal, then, is to face and process—to digest—this experience, but we are afraid that it will overwhelm us again as it did when the event first occurred. The primary purpose of therapy is to create a safe place: a caring, professional (meaning: trained and set within ethical boundaries) relationship. In the context of a safe relationship we approach the "emergency," the dangerous place. We seek together to face the troubling experience without being overwhelmed.

Therapy is only one kind of safe place. A "safe emergency" can happen anywhere we can find the combination of a safe relationship with the courage and intentionality of facing our pain. Even the shared pain of social injustice can be seen as requiring a safe place to face and explore the systems and structures that are keeping the injustice in place. In a way, this returns us to the first three responsive rhythms: in the context of celebration, lament and acceptance, we safely integrate a wounding experience.

A foundation for a safe relationship is that it be free of judgment and blame. Once a relationship has been established and trusted, however, many will benefit from discerning mistakes and unhealthy patterns together.

There are many other ways in which we help to create safety: giving full attention, giving appropriate time, offering discretion and trustworthiness, guarding against exploitation (using another for our own purposes), listening empathically and inviting others into ongoing community. When possible, affirming shared spiritual resources—such as acknowledging the loving presence of God—can also provide a key sense of safety.

Clearly the paths to healing for individuals are many and varied, and this is not the place to go into details. But a safe emergency, the experience that joins together a trusting relationship with the authentic integration of pain and suffering, is very often the context in which an incredibly wide range of healing can take place.

Intentionality

There has been some important conversation in recent years about how communities and individuals find direction. In a pluralistic world with so many choices and options, there is nothing obvious about knowing which way to go. While this chapter began by referring to a big-picture vision such as that associated with the word shalom, there can be a danger if too much focus is given to the destination. A vision of shalom is focused much more on how we are living the journey than on exactly what a hypothetical endpoint may look like.

What is crucial is having some intentionality about direction. Too much of society seems at present to be wandering aimlessly or stuck in ruts. If we are going to head down any new and positive path, we need guidance. Speaking of a vision of wholeness is only one way to do that. We can also focus on which way we start out or whose wisdom we are taking into account.

Without intentionality we are sitting ducks waiting to be manipulated by advertising and duped by propaganda. So once again we are reminded of the rhythmic nature of the journey together. We are intentional, but it takes wisdom to know when to hold the intentionality loosely and when to cling fiercely to a seemingly impossible hope. At times we will be guided by a picture of the way we imagine life together could be, and at times we let ourselves see when those visions are hurting people and getting in the way. We are steered by the wisdom of the past and the best creative voices in the present. We trust in our own ability to discern which way is best, but we also know that our discernment is far more reliable when shaped by a shared commitment to something much bigger than ourselves.

Getting Practical

Practise solidarity. If you're like most of us, you will find it easier to imagine solidarity with those with whom you share obvious similarities. Do you avoid imagining solidarity with certain groups of people? Those instantly justifying thoughts that go through your mind are a clue to the groups that you defend yourself against. Solidarity is both a perspective and an experience. If you are used to being in a privileged place in society, you won't find solidarity by serving meals at a soup kitchen. In fact, you may end up simply pitying the "poor souls" who march by. If you stick with it over time, this might change. But quicker results can come from making yourself dependent on people who are very different from you. So instead, if your roots are in Christian Europe, consider visiting a mosque—all the better if the language is different. Let yourself feel the dis-ease, the vulnerability and the visibility. That kind of experience can help you find a stance of solidarity with the marginalized around us.

Face pain. Think of the people that you spend the most time with: your closest friends and family. Do you have any means by which to create opportunities to hear each other's pain so that you can be a healing presence to each other? Or is it all too natural to avoid bringing such things up with each other? Know that if nothing painful has come up in the last few months or even years, it's not because there hasn't been anything painful. How can you create openness to "be there" for each other—to provide a "safe emergency" that will enable deep healing in the most natural context? Trying out the sharing of "highs and lows" as mentioned earlier could be a starting place.

Invite accountability. Many men (in particular) are familiar with accountability when it comes to asking a friend or mentor to support them as they give up an addiction like pornography or alcohol. But few of us invite accountability when we want support for making significant lifestyle changes. One way to live more intentionally without preaching to your friends is to ask for support from friends regarding a change that you want to make. For example, let's say you want to go car-free. You could ask friends if they would support this decision by "renting" their car to you on those few occasions when you need one (while making it clear that you are not hinting that they should offer you rides all the time). In this way you are seeking support and modelling change at the same time.

7 YEARNING FOR HOME

The whole idea of compassion is based on a keen awareness of the interdependence of all these living beings, which are all part of one another, and all involved in one another.

– Thomas Merton

"Well," said Pooh, "what I like best—" and then he had to stop and think. Because although Eating Honey was a very good thing to do, there was a moment just before you began to eat it which was better than when you were, but he didn't know what it was called. And then he thought that being with Christopher Robin was a very good thing to do, and having Piglet near was a very friendly thing to have; and so, when he had thought it all out, he said, "What I like best in the whole world is Me and Piglet going to see You, and You saying 'What about a little something?' and Me saying, 'Well, I shouldn't mind a little something, should you, Piglet,' and it being a hummy sort of day outside, and birds singing."

- A. A. Milne

Imagine a man in his mid-30s. Having spent his early adulthood chasing thrills, which included exotic short-term jobs, recreational sex and mild drug use, he begins to see that his future is looking lonely. Deep friendships are non-existent. One day, newly relocated in a large city, he calls up an old college friend and finds himself invited to supper in a rather seedy part of town. When he finds the right address, it's an oddly striking oasis that seems to exude light: a small, brick apartment block skillfully painted with colours as bright as the plentiful graffiti he passed on the way there. He finds out that his supper is "pot-luck," shared with all the residents of the building in a large community room on the main floor. There's a very mixed assortment of people ranging from idealistic young college students to a couple of elderly men who are clearly mentally ill. The food is of mixed quality as well. A skirmish breaks out at one end of the table that almost gets out of hand. But there is laughter. And people who, for the most part, are comfortable with each other. They seem glad he's there.

After a few weeks of regular visits, his friend invites him to become a part of the co-op that runs the building, and he finds himself agreeing with more enthusiasm than he would have guessed when he first drove through the neighbourhood. It isn't anything at all like the family he grew up in, but it's the first time in many years he's felt at home.

~

Having set out to explore the rhythms and practices that invite experiences of wholeness, I have thus far been fairly silent about what exactly wholeness is. In no small part this is due to my inadequacy for the task. I think the best I can do is to try to approach the question metaphorically and hope it points toward an answer.

Psychologically, some have spoken of the original wholeness of the womb. The unborn child is at one with its universe—its mother—and, we assume, experiences safety and connection. However, as a picture of wholeness, this has usually been considered something of a double-edged sword: the memory of the womb may evoke a sense of unity, but as a goal it is seen as regressive or even a death wish.

The metaphor or perhaps even archetype that I suggest instead is that of being held by an engaged, responsive parent who is looking at us with clear delight. Most essentially, we don't want to see concern (which in some cases might cause us anxiety) or a face that is set and determined to provide for our well-being or to fix us (which may look distant and disengaged); we want to see someone's joy at simply being in our presence. Perhaps we can perfect the picture if we think of an infant that has just finished breastfeeding or, reminiscent of the Pooh quote at the beginning of the chapter, that snuggles in against the breast in anticipation.

Like the womb metaphor, this could also be seen as regressive when considered as a goal, but now we are closer to an image that can be transformed into outward, socially mature parallels. For example, our sexual longings are almost certainly affected by such memories or images, but in the act of sex the regressive element (returning to the hunger for the breast and the intimacy of skin contact) is matched by its element of giving pleasure/nurture to another and of the mature longing to create new life.

More broadly speaking, the image of being held by a responsive parent speaks to our longing for relational engagement and for belonging in community. And, again, wholeness involves us in both roles of the metaphor. We long to experience the care and attention that the child receives, and we long to provide that nurture to, and delight in, others. As an archetype of wholeness, then, we imagine that wholeness is connected to such overlapping concepts as love, intimacy, vulnerability, connectedness, commitment and maturing responsibility.

Even when one experiences the kinds of moments that should fulfill these longings—a satisfying sexual experience with a loving partner, holding a smiling child in our arms, feeling accepted and finding a niche in a healthy community—we will often still feel a yearning for something more. This has often been interpreted as a spiritual hunger. Perhaps the best-known articulation of this is the words of St. Augustine: "Our hearts are restless until they find their rest in You."

For the sake of simplicity, I will draw both the original metaphor of the parent holding the child and all the complex concepts that are reflected in that image with its lifelong echoes, into the simpler metaphor of home. If the concept of home becomes too abstract at times, it is good to remember the tangible relationship between parent and child that is its root.

So this final rhythm is one that doesn't fit neatly into the first set of rhythms of response nor the second set of rhythms of action. The rhythm represented by our yearning for home is about settling down and about being unsettled. We are drawn out of the smallness—the isolation—of ourselves, of our families and communities, and we are led back toward the need for identity, commitment and belonging. The nature of the paradox grows deeper than ever.

There are all kinds of sights, sounds and smells in the world that can trigger a deep yearning for home. Perhaps the word "yearning" by itself communicates even more universally than the object, "home." For me, something like an abandoned homestead on the edge of an overgrown pasture can spark a deep, inexplicable longing. For others it might be seeing a tearful greeting as someone is met by loved ones at an airport. We just know we are yearning for something: peace, connection, joy, silence, God, an end to pain—or something that represents the possibility of all of the above.

The word "home" tends to evoke passionate or at least emotional responses inside us. It may represent a longing for the place where we know we belong, where we are loved and noticed. Or it may conjure up feelings of hurt, resentment or disappointment as we recall the brokenness of previous attempts at creating a home, or the despair of fearing that we will never find one. Some of us will feel mixtures of both.

Longings are created by what we have and haven't had. With varying degrees of what we believe is possible, we set out for home. We leave home, we search for home, we create homes together. The yearning that we feel even in the most settled of moments reminds us that home is never an entirely settled place, but a place that must allow and invite change—that encourages coming and going.

The paradoxes of love and family

There are deep paradoxes involved in our emotional attachments to the idea of home. We might ponder how we think of home as it refers to a small nuclear family. Loyalty among the closest levels of family has generally been the bedrock of all social organization. The deepest understandings of love have been those associated with the covenants and commitments that bind a family together in mutual care. Even when committed love extends beyond the borders of family, we often associate these feelings and attachments to family roots: we might say that we "love someone like a brother."

A family, a household, can make the experience of home immediate and tangible. Hopefully, within our homes we don't need to lock our doors for safety. A family often shares one economic purse and there is some ability to count on one another for practical and emotional support, though of course there are exceptions. The lives of family members are intertwined. For good or ill, they belong together and have a place.

Yet if our nuclear family defines the boundaries of home, then we are not at home the minute we step outside our front door. Overemphasis on deep loyalty and commitment within the family can quickly become justification for competition, violence and war with those outside. We might raise the question, "How far should our sense of family extend?" This is the subversive question that Jesus once asked: "Who is my mother, and who are my brothers?" (Matt. 12.48). Don't we long for the boundaries of home to open wide?

What if, as Thomas Merton suggested in the quote at the start of this chapter, we are "all involved in one another"? In order for an understanding of love to be pointed outward with unlimited expansive possibility, I would describe love as *the awareness of and commitment to the understanding that our well-being is bound up together with others. Thus, we are loyal not out of "charity" but out of mutual care. We see and delight in the unity of which we are becoming more aware.* As we go through life, we can keep on extending our awareness of all those with whom we are connected. Our idea of home gets bigger and bigger.

Of course, descriptions and definitions of love always fall short and sound thin because love is not only a cognitive awareness or an intentional commitment—it is something deeply felt and experienced. Love is seeing someone and knowing in my gut that this person is a part of me; we are, together, a beautiful unity. The highest forms of love are often understood to be self-sacrificing, but this sacrifice is not because of any self-denigration. Rather, it is because we understand deeply that our sacrifice is for the good of the whole of which we are a part.

Drawing a bigger and bigger net around what becomes home for us does not mean that all is pleasant and uncomplicated. After all, the small family home can contain anger and hurt, even hatred. The mutual participation, the interconnectedness, makes love emotional in negative as well as positive ways. The interdependence, and the vulnerability that comes with it, means that when fear and frustrated desire enter the picture, we can easily convert the powerful emotions of love into hatred toward those we are linked with that cause us pain. Who would bother to waste the energy required to hate on those with whom one is not connected? Hatred alerts us to the desperate need to regain a sense of safety and trust, or, sadly, drives us to find ways to reject those with whom we no longer feel we can remain vulnerable. It is not without risk that we invite more of humanity to become family.

So, on the one hand, developing an expansive sense of home connects us with more and more of the world outside of our doors. We realize that our town is our home, our nation is our home, the planet is our home.

On the other hand, an expansive sense of home tends toward the abstract and mystical, and we need love to be embodied. We have to guard against the temptation to hide behind our relatively hypothetical love for people at a great distance as a way to neglect our difficulty with loving those close to us. The tension between the poles of this dialectic needs to be maintained. Safely inside our households, we yearn for a bigger sense of home; mystically aware of the mutual connection with the universe, we yearn for the touch of a particular relationship.

Exclusivity and inclusivity

Most of us would agree that the most intimate, embodied love requires a sense of exclusivity. While in some ways love and mutuality can sometimes be shared in a very inclusive way, the deepest experience of vulnerability and reciprocity necessitates a unique and exclusive loyalty to our spouses and partners. Our need for belonging and for finding a confident part of our identity in particular relationships requires boundaries, exclusivity. It must *mean something* unique to be married; it must *mean something* to be committed to a community. To be betrayed physically is a deep blow to any marriage, but how much deeper still when a spouse gives his or her intimate loyalty to another, when the meaning of a marriage is at least temporarily destroyed?

The longing to create this exclusive love is what we usually call romantic love. This uniquely emotional form of love has such great highs and lows of feeling that psychologists' descriptions of romance often make it sound like an illness. As we most typically tell stories about it, romance is exclusive love that is in question: the longing and suspense about whether I can bind myself to another in whom I see the deep potential to fulfill a lack in myself. I can feel such love not only for a person but for a community or a place—for belonging and home. Aren't romantic love and the longing for home very nearly the same? Only the thinnest and emptiest of lust has removed from sexual desire all of those longings to nest and create home. Only empty, sterile sex removes from the joining of bodies the hope that this act begins or continues something profoundly shared. Once one is securely nested in a faithful relationship or community, the feeling of being "in love" is probably more akin to delight than what is usually called romance with its urgent and insecure longings.

When trust and faithfulness are established at the core of a relationship like a marriage, a freer openness to community is enabled; exclusivity in marriage can enable rather than hinder the inclusivity of community. When trust is deep and commitments are protected, we have a foundation on which to build meaningful relationships with others. The paradox keeps rippling outward in concentric circles: a certain kind of loyalty to one's local community helps rather than hinders the best mutuality with distant communities and the larger human family.

Without care, however, the dark side of this paradox can become an excuse for selfishness. My loyalty to my spouse and family should not permit me to work for the comfort and protection of my family *at the expense of* or *to the undue neglect of* others whom I also love, though at a greater distance. There are times when a parent rightly leads a family into shared sacrifice or risk for the sake of others. A parent may give up a well-paying job in order to choose work that is less exploitative of the planet or the developing world. As a result, there is no college fund and the kids have fewer toys than their neighbours.

There are other times when this sacrifice seems inappropriate. I have seen children who have suffered as a result of parents who, out of what seems like unbalanced love, did not adequately protect their family. There are saintly foster parents who have cared for dozens of the most needy children while neglecting their own children's needs. There are heroic individuals who have travelled the world to care for the poorest of the poor while their family falls apart back home. This is a balance that is fraught with peril.

Similarly, loyalty to a local community requires a balance in relation to loyalty to larger extensions of the human family. It may seem counterintuitive, but many voices wise in global issues have encouraged activists to look first to their local community. Healthy local communities are much less inclined to exploit distant ones. Instead, each community, near and far, can make a more positive contribution to the earth's environment or the global economy when they look wisely to their own interests. Yet we must recall that terrible things have been done by self-serving industrial nations or by tribes tucked away in hidden forests—whenever human groups have seen outsiders as less human and less worthy than themselves.

Spiritual exclusivity and inclusivity

Humanity has grown weary of wars justified by religious differences. Even when holy books speak of love and peace, adherents have chosen to slaughter those who believe in different holy books. We know this is insane. Where does this leave us in seeking a spiritual home? Is there any room left for commitment and loyalty to competing stories about God?

It is said that the Judeo-Christian God is a jealous god. If the grounds of that notion are an understanding of a god who is insecure and controlling, we would be right in outgrowing the belief. But perhaps the ancient idea is for our protection. Perhaps we need loyal trust in a living God that cannot be shared or exchanged, when convenient, with lesser, imitation gods—that is, by putting ultimate trust in human rationality, pleasure, wealth, power or pride in our own supposed infallibility. Too often, individuals, groups and even nations have tried to blend worship of these tiny "gods" with that of a living and mysterious God, to great harm and detriment. Always, these false unions grossly distort the understanding of God, as people attempt to make the mystery of God into a tool for their own manipulations or pretend to know absolutely what they have only glimpsed. Perhaps a jealous God, unfathomable and beyond manipulation, is one who is trying to protect us from any commitments that are too small.

I don't see a healthy religious commitment as justifying an arrogant or closed attitude toward other faiths. In fact, I would have no interest in a God who is not the God of all, and that must mean that no single community can be given sole power to define or reveal God. The Hebrew Bible freely used the words *El* or *Elohim* for God in spite of those being the names used for god(s) by other cultures. The Aramaic word for God used by Jesus can be transliterated as *Elah* or *Alah*, nearly identical with the Arabic *Allah* used today by Muslims (and, of course, both are referring to the God of Abraham). We've seen Christians needing to be reminded about the nonviolence of Jesus through the Hindu, Gandhi. In the '60s and '70s, American Christians (like Thomas Merton and James Douglass) were inspired in their understandings of the spiritual contemplation needed to undergird the resistance to the Vietnam War by the Buddhist, Thich Nhat Hanh. In Nigeria, an important interfaith movement trying to stop the violence between Christians and Muslims was started when Imam Muhammed Ashafa responded to the teaching on forgiveness in his mosque and approached his enemy, Pastor James Wuye. Christians have often needed the help of people of other faiths to be reminded of what is within their own book, which teaches that God is revealed to all humanity.

The manipulative use of man-made gods is what generates the harshest critiques in the Bible. If we maintain a healthy awareness of what is knowable and what is beyond knowable about God, we can remain open and respectful, with all faiths seen as potentially revealing something new about the mystery of God and human spirituality.

Specific religious commitments are important in linking us to life-giving traditions and to tangible communities that shape our lives. But these commitments must be held in tension with a dedication to appropriate inclusivity toward those with whom we are also connected in larger, more universal, ways. When individuals are narrowly committed to only one small community, for example, they are trapped in a small world. The limited and occasionally distorted worldview of a community (varying, of course, according to the health of the community) will harden into the fixed reality of the member whose perspective is not challenged by outside perspectives. This is a key reason why hospitality to the stranger is so crucial. We must remain open to outside perspectives.

Love and loyalty in multiple communities

In our present society, we can scarcely avoid the need to be part of multiple communities. We may feel an important part of a workplace community, a faith community, a neighbourhood or town, a political organization, a sports league or an extended family. The rough edges of competing loyalties can be challenging. We can feel fragmented and disoriented by the differing points of view.

In order to thrive in this context of multiple communities, we need to develop an inner strength, which psychologists use a variety of terms to describe, like individuation, differentiation or integration. These are complex concepts, but they all involve individuals in a process of discerning which aspects of their relational lives to internalize and which aspects from which they need to separate. This enables us to accept a degree of dependence on others while simultaneously limiting that dependence when necessary to preserve flexibility and the freedom to grow. We know that we are making progress when we become less reactive emotionally to those who disagree with us and when we can tolerate and accept our own inner conflicts.

Theorists like James Fowler and others have described a similar process regarding how we develop spiritually. Growing into a mature faith requires that we allow seasons of questioning and thinking critically about what we believe. What emerges is a confidence in a faith that is broad and resilient enough to contain tensions and paradoxes. For some, this means that a rigid literalism gives way to a metaphorical depth of understanding.

Whether viewed psychologically or spiritually, this development of inner, individual strength, of resilient identity, is what enables healthy membership in communities. Experience in various relational contexts is part of the path and the destination on this journey.

I am very grateful for all the shifts and upheavals that have taken place in my understandings over the years, partly because of the various contexts I have been in. Perspectives from family and spiritual communities have clashed with academic and professional insights, and in the end I have been enriched by the battle. I hope I have somehow remained appropriately loyal to family, church and academia. We need the perspectives of many communities to reach the best understanding of truth.

How well we are individually able to manage this paradox of exclusivity and inclusivity, of loyalty and belonging in several directions at once, will depend very much on the health of the communities of which we're a part. Perhaps surprising to some, communities that are experienced as particularly close and loving are not necessarily the communities that do well over long periods of time. "Cooler" communities have more potential to thrive longer. It would appear that the emotional intensity and intimacy present in "warmer" communities tend to create boundary issues (people do not feel free to leave or are treated as traitors when they do), and such communities seldom survive a change in charismatic leadership.

Perhaps the worst of all is a community with origins in a time of great closeness and dependence, loyally centred on a charismatic leader, which eventually hardens into a rigid and controlling community with expectations based on fear. Such a community will usually do all in its power to stop its members from being inclusive toward outsiders or from dividing their loyalty with other communities. They realize, perhaps rightly, that their community might collapse if seen in the light of fresh perspectives or changed circumstances.

Healthy communities encourage an open-handed loyalty. There is a genuine loyalty expected, and accountability can take place, but there is also a respect for individuals' personal boundaries and a willingness to accept competing loyalties and commitments to other groups. The community's own boundaries are permeable;[4] they are visible enough to create a sense of belonging or identity, but they are open enough that people can come and go without the community feeling threatened.

While we may associate the small and controlling kind of community with those we refer to as cults, it is quite common even for more mainstream communities to treat their grown children as traitors when they return from university unable to believe the narrow and rigid teachings that define the group.

Biology teaches us that cross-pollination produces "hybrid vigour." There is creativity generated when the ideas of different communities meet to produce new possibilities. In recent years, the field of psychotherapy has been energized by the introduction

---

[4] A word common in biology for cell membranes that do a surprisingly efficient job of letting appropriate things in and out, while still maintaining a cell's integrity.

of the concept of mindfulness from the Buddhists. Protestants have deepened their spiritual lives by practising Catholic Ignatian exercises. Huge movements of people in the developing world have found a new joy in the songs and prayers of Charismatic and Pentecostal traditions.

I would even go so far as to say that if our loyalty extends to only one community, and is not balanced by some level of real engagement with others with contrasting values, perspectives and understandings, that single community will tend to become like a controlling tyrant to us. Too much power of meaning, belonging and identity is tied up in that single centre, and its hold over us is too great. Few communities are healthy enough to thrive under such conditions of concentrated power.

More typically, we navigate a sense of home based on the complexity of multiple communities. This adds a rich tension to our lives that helps prevent our getting stuck in too narrow a perspective. The healthy community honours this diversity in spite of the potential unsettledness it causes.

The depths of wounded hearts

In the 21st century, most of us have grown used to a multicultural landscape, and we manage the diversity at the peripheries of life relatively well. Often, the hardest part of love and loyalty are with those closest to our cores. The relationships in which we experience our deepest belonging, our lived-out identities—the people and groups that we most rely on to meet our daily needs and to which we open up our most vulnerable selves— are our psychological "holy of holies." Our deepest and most hidden selves are bound up with these relationships. With roots in our earliest relational experiences, good and bad, our unconscious emotions have been formed to guard this inner sacred place.

While there are ancient spiritual and philosophical references to these barely known depths of the heart, it was Freud who really focused attention on what goes on inside people at this buried level. And as most of us know, Freud discussed the unconscious primarily in sexual terms. Many of his followers since, however, have wisely realized that it is not so much sex *per se,* but close, secure and embodied relationships that are at stake here. Our earliest selves are completely dependent on being held and nurtured. Since most parenting is very inconsistent and the challenges of life can impinge on this early care, we also learn the ways in which these deepest needs become interrupted and distorted.

As a result we are all, more or less, wounded during these earliest years. For some, the minor wounds that arise are healed or overcome by the overall security of relationships we have and the acceptance that is usually expressed. For many others, the wounds, small or large, linger and shape our future relating. We have been given "unfinished business" that will express itself in our closest relationships.

Of course, intimate love that is strongly flavoured by our sexuality will be the love most affected by our unfinished business. Even in the healthiest romantic relationships, an unconscious or fantasy love coexists with a conscious, more rational attraction. The fantasy-based side fuels unconscious energy and desire, while the reality-based side helps ground and nurture a realistically life-giving relationship. Both sides are positive and important when kept in an integrated balance. The fantasy side is easily visible in the exaggerated (but possibly beautiful) imagery of love songs, while practical wisdom keeps an eye open for things like mutual interests, values and a healthy balance of give and take.

Unfortunately the unconscious side also creates unhelpful expectations and fears, which greatly interfere with both new and established relationships. Early in my family counselling practice, I read a theory that suggested that we are often unconsciously attracted to someone who is in some way deeply familiar to us. Something speaks of home to our inner being—with its positive sense *and* with the threat of repeating some of the wounding that we received from one or both of our parents. So, a young girl with an absent father who rarely paid attention to her later becomes attracted to the young man whose attention she has to win but who is otherwise at least a little absent like her father was. This theory is not as pessimistic as it sounds, as it also suggests that what really makes this romantic attraction sizzle is when there are signs of hope that within this new relationship, the old wound might be opened but also overcome and healed. In marriage counselling, the hope is that the latter possibility is realized.

Romance is only one of the places affected by unfinished business and emotions birthed in unconscious memories. Our close friendships and our most central communities will also be much affected. We unnecessarily and unhelpfully test our friends, expecting that they might betray us at the least sign of our weakness. We project all kinds of positive and negative parental expectations (transference) on our community's leaders. A community can be torn apart when a perceived betrayal suddenly makes the situation seem unsafe for some individual or subgroup. Relationships in which we find belonging and identity are fraught with messiness because they touch the core of our being. The same dynamic that allows communities to be deeply healing is the one that makes them messy and painful. They expose our hearts.

Safe communities and healing relationships are ones that expect messiness and are committed and open in response to, and irrespective of, that messiness. If occasional moments get reactive and intense, there is also an ability to communicate and address hurts before battle lines harden. They are relatively faithful, persistent and trustworthy through the ups and downs of life. They can tolerate the emergence of "unfinished business" and provide a context in which processing, integrating and healing can eventually take place.

This kind of love also needs to be embodied. It should be obvious—but enough groups have fallen into the trap that it's worth mentioning—that this community love cannot happen safely in sexualized ways. Communities that have experimented with free love and the sharing of partners have not proven themselves to be safe or enduring over time. Love in community is embodied by being practical and concrete: eating together, crying together, paying attention to each other. They provide hugs and appropriate touch; they help with moving and economic crises; they are present to give support when someone is sick or dying. All of these embodied expressions of love provide healing for the heart.

One of the more significant, small yet vital aspects of this embodiment is represented in greetings and partings. These are crucial markers of being home, of our belonging in community. If no one greets us upon arrival or notices our exit, how will we deeply believe that we belong? A very simple starting place to deepen our sense of community can come from paying more attention to noticing and greeting our family members when they come home, our colleagues when they arrive at work, our teammates when they drive up to the ball field.

Likewise, when we see someone headed for the door, it really matters if we call out a recognition of their leaving, or even express some appropriate affection. When these things are missed, we tend to feel that we don't matter to others. Yet, sometimes our insecurities and past disappointments make us collude with this invisibility by not approaching others for a greeting or by slinking away from a group.

We all need to be both givers and receivers of this embodied love. We learn how in community and find our unique gifts through experimenting and the encouragements of others. A home is not a perfect place, nor are communities meant to be as idealistic as this description may sound. What is required is intentionality, commitment and risk taking, combined with forgiveness and reconciliation for those many times when we all fall short. When we catch ourselves noticing glimpses of a good life, this kind of community will usually not be very far away.

Mystery

Whether or not we feel connected in relationships and communities, most of us will still know those moments when we ache for something more, perhaps not even knowing what we want. How often do we encounter something that triggers this yearning but is too vague to mean anything at all specific: a natural phenomenon like an unusually starry night, a song with lyrics that we can't interpret, a painting that prompts an un-nameable feeling?

Acknowledgment of the fundamental mystery at the core of the universe is the guarantee that we will never finally arrive at home to stay—at least not in any way that our present experience could help us understand. Instead, moments of feeling at home are a resting place until, in the face of renewed mystery, we are compelled to set out once again. If the journey didn't contain a possibility of home, it wouldn't be worth beginning. But if being home didn't retain some sense of mystery that instills restlessness and wonder, it wouldn't be worth staying.

Getting Practical

Map your communities. Think of several communities that you are a part of in the broadest sense of the word (consider extended family, churches, sports leagues, workplaces, civic organizations, etc.). How much diversity do they represent? How much overlap is there? Are any of them antagonistic? What happens to you when loyalties clash? How does your involvement in each give you a breadth and gift that you wouldn't have if you were only in one? Do you bring the blessings of one community into another? Is there any chance that one community is too "idolatrous"—as if it were a god in itself? Would you benefit by intentionally developing another community involvement?

Experiment with greetings and partings. For a few days (or a week if you have a long attention span), experiment with paying particular attention to greetings and partings. At first, just notice them: what are typical greetings and partings in your life looking like right now? Then practise making them more intentional. How does that seem to affect you and others?

Deal with unfinished business. Consider where you have recently run into problems with relationships. Is this related to any pattern that you have seen? Were the emotions that you felt in that situation similar to any that you felt strongly in your early life, or is the perceived hurt that you felt similar? Journal or talk to someone safe about the ways in which unfinished business might be imposing itself on the present or hindering the search for resolution.

Address the balance. Consider whether it is more typical for you to be the one giving or the one receiving love in your community. If you are normally receiving, what are some simple and concrete ways that you can demonstrate caring to someone in your community? Commit yourself to at least one such act very soon. If you are more normally giving, what are some ways in which you could share a need or make yourself more available to be cared for? Might you find a friend with whom to be more vulnerable? Could you ask for a lift, a helping hand or to borrow a tool instead of being self-sufficient?

Conclusion

A topic as big as wholeness will never become clear and straightforward, and none of us is whole enough to be entirely confident about what it looks like. Wholeness contains innumerable paradoxes and contradictions, tensions held in balance, rhythms and seasons that do not look alike. Yet there do seem to be some key aspects to these rhythms that are true across the diversity of humanity.

The seven rhythms I've described are my attempt to categorize the central elements of wholeness. My hope is that this model can provide a more inclusive understanding of what it means to be whole, that it can help us to imagine what a good life might look like in a way that is accessible and close at hand for everyone.

In the rhythms of response, I have described how the combination of celebrating, lamenting and accepting enable us to develop a well-rounded response to all of life. When none of these channels is blocked, we can engage deeply with reality with all of the resources that are a part of being human. Communities that encourage us with practices in each of these areas are crucial in order to equip us to deal with all of the joys and challenges of life.

The rhythms of action suggest that when we find and choose good work, when we can embrace the other, and when we are able to set out on the journey together, we become participants and partners in the nurture and transformation of our world.

The final rhythm, the yearning for home, proposes that we are drawn to belonging and rest, but also energized to continue searching by the mysterious sense that there is something more. We may never arrive at a place called wholeness, but we may find many glimpses of it along the way.

ACKNOWLEDGEMENTS

This book represents samples from a long journey of searching for the conditions in which wholeness can develop for individuals and communities. Therefore the contributors have been countless. The search began, in part, when I realized that most people hadn't experienced the kind of love and faithfulness that characterized the family in which I grew up, and so my gratitude begins there. It's amazing when adulthood hits and you realize that siblings can become friends. My brother, Vic, in particular became a partner in the adventure that took us out to New Brunswick, and this is typical of the way that he has helped me to see more of what is possible.

Once in New Brunswick, we were welcomed especially by Peter and Mary Ellen Fitch, who made it seem like they were just waiting for us to arrive. Their constant demonstration of love and passionate faith have been the core of the communities that have meant the most to me, and I only wish that more of their example would keep rubbing off on me.

So much of my life has been shaped by the students, staff and faculty of St. Stephen's University - in the classroom, around the lunch table, or on the road in Europe or Asia. I wish everyone could be a part of that kind of shared learning. Our faith community at the St. Croix Vineyard has provided a great example of the integration that is possible between ancient beliefs and a contemporary world. Sitting around the table with the likes of Rachael and Jeremy Barham, Gary and Helen Soucoup, Agnes and Andy Kramer-Hamstra, Ray and Rosie Funk eating consistently amazing food, drinking fair (let's be honest) wine, and basking in rich, honest and creative conversation has fed my spirit.

A wide variety of authors of fiction and non-fiction have shaped my thoughts, only a fraction of which are mentioned. I've had many teachers who have shaped me and my thoughts with their character and their ideas - among those whose ideas are reflected in this book are Gord Matties and Al Dueck.

Getting more specifically to this written project: Joel Mason (the man "glimpsing wholeness" in the cover photo) and Katie Gorrie have inspired and encouraged me by pioneering the Celtic Service with us and then by helping goad an attempt at writing to the point of completion (what a new thought!). Katie has then invested many hours of reading drafts and pointing me toward some directions and away from others—invaluable help for which I'm very grateful. Many students have read previous drafts and commented, and I've also appreciated feedback from Vic Thiessen, Peter Fitch and Daniel Thiessen on earlier drafts. Nancy Warren has then graciously reviewed and tweaked what has remained, and, of course, I take responsibility for whatever errors or crazy ideas have lingered on these pages.

Finally, my favourite community is the family my wife, Carol, and I have created. Rebekah, Cara (thanks for the cover!) and Daniel have all made the task of parenting a delight and tolerated well all the ideas and experiments that we tried out at home. Among those experiments has been sharing our home with others—much more often than not—and I also thank all of those temporary family members. Carol has been a more complete partner in life than I could have ever imagined. Her encouragement of my studies and writing have always been very tangible as she covered for all the other tasks around home that I have left undone. (Sorry for the hours of hiding behind my screen and thanks for often coaxing me away from it.)

FURTHER READING

On Celebrating

Capon, R. F. (2002). *The Supper of the Lamb*. Modern Library.
Doherty, W. J. (1999). *The Intentional Family*. William Morrow.
Emmons, R. (2007). *Thanks*. Houghton Mifflin Harcourt.
Lamott, A. (2012). *Help, Thanks, Wow*. Riverhead.
Taylor, B. B. (2009). *An Altar in the World*. HarperOne.
Wilson-Hartgrove, J. (2012). *The Awakening of Hope*. Zondervan.

On Lamenting

Brueggemann, W. (2007). *Praying the Psalms*. (2nd ed.). Cascade Books.
Herman, J. (1992). *Trauma and Recovery*. Basic.
Lewis, C. S. (1961). *A Grief Observed*. Faber and Faber.
Swinton, J. (2007). *Raging With Compassion*. Eerdmans.
Wiman, C. (2013). *My Bright Abyss*. Farrar, Straus and Giroux.
Wolterstorff, N. (1987). *Lament for a Son*. Eerdmans.
Yancey, P. (1988). *Disappointment with God*. Zondervan.

On Accepting

Brown, Brene. (2012). *Daring Greatly*. Gotham.
Enright, R. D. (2001). *Forgiveness Is a Choice*. American Psychological Association.
Hanh, T. N. (1999). *The Miracle of Mindfulness*. (M. Ho, Trans.) Beacon Press.

Lawrence, B. *The Practice of the Presence of God*. Various – 17th Century.
May, G. (1988). *Addiction and Grace*. HarperCollins.
Rohr, R. (1999). *Everything Belongs*. Crossroad.
Smedes, L. B. (1997). *The Art of Forgiving*. Ballantine.
Thurman, H. (1984). *For the Inward Journey*. Friends United.
Vanier, J. (2008). *Becoming Human (2nd ed.)*. Paulist Press.

On Good Work

Berry, W. (2010a). *What Matters?* Counterpoint.
Berry, W. (2010b). *What Are People For?* (2nd ed.). Counterpoint.
Boers, A. (2012). *Living into Focus*. Brazos.
Borgmann, A. (2003). *Power Failure*. Brazos.
Fox, M. (1995). *The Reinvention of Work*. HarperOne.
Muller, W. (2000). *Sabbath*. Bantam.
Palmer, P. J. (1999). *The Active Life*. Jossey-Bass.
Schumacher, E. F. (1979). *Good Work*. HarperCollins.
Schumacher, E. F. (1973, 2010). *Small Is Beautiful* (Reprint). Harper Perennial.
Weil, S. and Miles, S. (2000). *Simone Weil: An Anthology*. Grove.

On Embracing the Other

Beck, R. (2012). *Unclean*. Lutterworth Press.
Buber, M. (1971). *I And Thou*. (W. Kaufmann, Trans.). Touchstone.
Pohl, C. D. (2011). *Living into Community*. Eerdmans.
Rifkin, J. (2009). *The Empathic Civilization*. Tarcher.

Vanier, J. (2006). *Encountering "the Other."* Paulist Press.

Volf, M. (1996). *Exclusion & Embrace.* Abingdon Press.

On Journeying Together

Berry, W. (1993). *Sex, Economy, Freedom & Community.* Pantheon.

Claiborne, S. (2006). *The Irresistible Revolution.* Zondervan.

Cozolino, L. (2010). *The Neuroscience of Psychotherapy.* W. W. Norton & Co.

Heschel, A. J. (2007). The Prophets. Hendrickson.

Loeb, P. R. (2004). *The Impossible Will Take a Little While.* Basic.

MacIntyre, A. (2007 [1981]). *After Virtue, 3rd ed.* University of Notre Dame Press.

McLaren, B. (2009). *Everything Must Change.* Thomas Nelson.

Merton, T. (1968). *Conjectures of a Guilty Bystander.* Image.

Nouwen, H. J. M. (1979). *The Wounded Healer.* Image.

Peck, M. S. (1983). *People of the Lie.* Touchstone.

Weil, S. (2001 [1949]). *The Need for Roots.* Routledge.

Wink, W. (1999). *The Powers That Be.* Three Rivers.

On Yearning for Home

Bonhoeffer, D. (1978). *Life Together.* HarperOne.

Cloud, H., & Townsend, J. (1992). *Boundaries.* (Revised). Zondervan.

McLaren, B. (2012). *Why did Jesus, Moses, the Buddha, and Mohammed Cross the Road?* Jericho.

Palmer, P. J. (1993). *To Know as We Are Known.* HarperOne.

Putnam, R. (2000). *Bowling Alone*. Simon & Schuster.

Taylor, B. B. (2007). *Leaving Church*. HarperOne.

Vanier, J. (1989). *Community and Growth* (2nd Revised). Paulist Press.

Vanier, J. (2008). *Becoming Human* (2nd ed.). Paulist Press.

Join the ongoing conversation:

www.glimpsesofagoodlife.com

www.ingramcontent.com/pod-product-compliance
Lightning Source LLC
Chambersburg PA
CBHW051652040426
42446CB00009B/1096